BOYS'

DEVOTIONAL

BIBLE
DEVOTIONS
for
PRETEEN BOYS
AGED 10-12

by

ANDERS BENNETT

ADISAN Publishing AB

Table of Contents

Introduction

Even at a young age, you already understand that life isn't always easy. Things can go wrong, and some events in life can be very hard to face. That's why it's important to keep yourself close to God. Remember, you are never alone. God is always with you to guide you and help you grow into an honorable, humble, and God-loving man.

This book aims to help you walk with God every day. As you read His word, you'll begin to understand how God works in different aspects of your life. You'll learn what it means to be a young Christian in this world, and you can live your life according to God's perfect plan. He will give you the strength to meet any challenge.

He will guide you along the right path. So, I invite you to take on this journey and draw a little closer to God today. Spend a few minutes reading and meditating on God's word every day. Seek His guidance, and you'll be amazed at how He works so marvelously in your life and in the lives of people around you.

PART 1

Finding My Real Value

Created for a Purpose

"What is man that you are mindful of him, and the son of man that you care for him? Yet you have made him a little lower than the heavenly beings and crowned him with glory and honor."
Psalm 8:4-5, ESV

We all have times when we feel like we're not good enough. Maybe someone made a mean comment, or you see other kids doing things that make you feel inferior. If you ever feel like this, remember that you are created in God's own image.

You are only a little lower than the magnificent, powerful angels! God has a beautiful plan for your life. He has given you life with an important purpose in His Kingdom.

He created you with a unique personality. You have been given gifts and talents by God that are unique to you. No one else has the exact same combination of gifts and talents that you have. You may not be aware of every gift God has given you yet. But as you grow and discover more things, you'll be amazed at your God-given talents.

So, when you feel like you are less than special, remember the gifts and talents that God has given you. But most of all, remember that God loves you so much there is nothing He won't do to draw you closer to His side. He even gave up His most treasured and perfect son, Jesus, for you.

Day 2

Born with so much Potential

"For I know the plans I have for you, declares the Lord, plans for welfare and not for evil, to give you a future and a hope."
Jeremiah 29:11, ESV

Have you ever wondered why God created you? You may not realize it, but God has a special plan for you. He knit you together in your mother's womb and knew you by name before you were even born.

God made you because He wants you to develop a close relationship with Him. He loves you so much that He wants you to know Him! Also, He wants to mold you to reflect His image.

Imagine being like Jesus himself! You can be like Him if you walk closely with him and know Him for who He is. By reading the Bible, praying, and obeying Him, you can learn so much about God and know His will in your life. And if you follow God's perfect plan for your life, you can achieve amazing things which you probably never imagined.

Always follow God's voice, expressed in His word. And if you grow closer to Him, you will also know the voice of the Holy Spirit in your heart.

So, don't waste any time worrying about what you're supposed to do or where you're supposed to go. Instead, ask God to reveal His plan for your life and then trust that He will guide you every step of the way.

BOYS

BIBLE

DEVOTIONS

Day 3

Focusing on my Strengths

*"Having gifts that differ according to the
grace given to us, let us use them..."*
Romans 12:6, ESV

God has given everyone his or her own unique set of skills and strengths. However, it can be easy to get caught up in comparison and start feeling like you're not as good as your friends or family members.

Maybe you're not as smart or as good at sports as your friends. But that doesn't make you less special than they are. You may not know all of your strengths yet, but God has given you a unique set of talents and skills, which you can use for His glory.

If you're wondering how you can best serve God and His Kingdom, a good place to start is by looking at the skills and strengths He has given you. You can try different things to discover what you like or are good at.

Once you have a better idea of your gifts, you can start thinking about how to use them to serve God and His people. Maybe there's a need in your church or community that you can help meet. Maybe you can use your gifts to reach out to those who don't yet know Christ.

Whatever it is, God will give you the
strength and ability to do it if you ask Him.
So don't be afraid to step out in faith and
use the gifts He's given you for His glory.

Day 4

Working on Your Weaknesses

*But He said to me, "My grace is sufficient for you,
for power is perfected in weakness." Therefore, I will
most gladly boast all the more about my weaknesses,
so that Christ's power may reside in me.*
2 Corinthians 12:9, HCSB

Have you ever tried something and failed? Failure can make you feel discouraged, and it's okay. But despite mistakes and disappointments, you should never focus on your weaknesses. That's because your weaknesses are an opportunity for God to work in your life. God can take these weaknesses and use them to make you a stronger person.

So, how do you turn your weakness into a strength? First, admit your weaknesses. Be honest about where you need help and hand them over to God. Next, pray for strength.

When you pray, you invite God into the situation and ask for His power to work in your life. As you surrender your weaknesses to God, He will begin to work in you and give you the strength you need to overcome them.

You may not be able to fix everything overnight. But if you take small steps and keep moving forward, you will get there eventually. Most importantly, always remember that you are not alone in this journey. God is always with us, and He will be your source of strength to face every challenge in life.

BOYS

BIBLE

DEVOTIONS

Day 5

Finding Your Spiritual Gifts

"Each of you should use whatever gift you have received to serve others, as faithful stewards of God's grace in its various forms."
1 Peter 4:10, NIV

The Bible talks about spiritual gifts in a few different places. In 1 Corinthians 12, Paul lists some of the gifts that are available to Christians, including prophecy, teaching, wisdom, knowledge, faith, healing, and miracles. And in Romans 12, he talks about how each Christian has been given a unique gift or talent to use for the good of the church.

So what exactly are spiritual gifts? They are supernatural abilities that God gives to Christians to help them serve HIM and others. These gifts are not just for personal benefit or enjoyment; they are meant to be used to build up the body of Christ and advance God's Kingdom.

If you're not sure what your spiritual gifts are, don't worry! There are many ways to find out. The first thing to do is to ask God to reveal them to you. Another way to discover your spiritual gifts is by asking your pastor or other church leaders about what they see you can do.

You will be surprised to find that you are actually able to do something you never thought you could! Finally, always remember that these gifts are not about YOU; they're about glorifying God and serving His people. So don't be afraid to ask for help in finding your place in HIS work.

Embracing Your Unique Personality

"I praise you because I am fearfully and wonderfully made; Your works are wonderful, I know that full well."
Psalm 139:14, NIV

Most people want to be unique and different from everyone else. They do this by dying their hair in strange colors or by wearing different types of clothes to set themselves apart. But we don't really need to try so hard to look unique because we are all created by God, each with unique characteristics and personalities.

Our fingerprints, footprints, voice patterns, and DNA all prove how unique each of us is. So, never try to change your physical appearance or your personality just to be somebody else. Look at yourself and understand how God created you that way.

You may not see your real beauty right now, but you are beautiful! Your hair is never too straight nor too curly. Your skin color is never too dark or too light. If you're funny, then feel free to cheer people up. If you like the quiet, that's great too!

You are uniquely you, and God designed you as you are because He knows your body and your personality are just right! Don't try to copy someone else, no matter how cool you think they are, because anyone different from yourself is already taken!

As God's child, you don't have to be someone else to be accepted God already loves you so much! Wear your body with confidence because you are fearfully and wonderfully made!

BOYS

BIBLE

DEVOTIONS

PART 2

Becoming a Christian

Seeking God

"Now this is eternal life: that they know you, the only true God, and Jesus Christ, whom you have sent."
John 17:3, NIV

Jesus tells us that eternal life is found in knowing God. This means that the most important thoughts we can have are the ones that are about God. It's our responsibility and privilege as Christians to seek Him every day. And what better way to get to know God than reading His precious Word- The Bible!

When you read the Bible, you can learn what He's like, what He's done, and what He has planned for your life. As you read, ask God for heavenly wisdom, so you will understand what God is teaching you about Himself.

Another important way to know God is by talking to Him in prayer. Prayer is a two-way conversation, so while you share your thoughts and desires with God, don't forget to listen for His response as well.

Finally, you can also know and enjoy who God is by spending time with other Christians and learning how God works in their people's lives.

God loves to reveal Himself in His word, in our lives, and especially in His creation. So let's make an effort to do those things each day so that we can better know our heavenly Father!

BOYS

BIBLE

DEVOTIONS

Day 8

Loving God Above All

"Jesus replied: 'Love the Lord your God with all your heart and with all your soul and with all your mind.'"
Matthew 22:37, NIV

We all have different things that are important to us. For some, it might be their friends and families. Others can be very passionate about sports, music, and other things they enjoy. But no matter what you love, always remember to put God first in your life.

As Jesus said, the greatest commandment is that we love God with our all. That's because He is God, and He is the only one who is worthy of our worship. However, because of our sinful nature, we often find ourselves breaking this very first commandment, and we worship anyone or anything other than Him.

You probably think you have never worshipped a different God. But sadly, every time you put someone or something above God, you are committing idolatry.

So, how do you make sure you obey God's most important commandment? You'll need to make a decision to love Him above all and to choose him above everything else.

Loving God also means obeying Him and striving to live according to His will. So if you want to love God above all, start by making the decision to love Him today. Then take some time to get to know Him better through prayer and study. As you do, your love for Him will grow deeper and stronger each day.

Christ's Sacrifice

*"For God so loved the world that he gave his
one and only Son, that whoever believes in him
shall not perish but have eternal life."*
John 3:16, NIV

We serve a holy God. Although He is overflowing with love for us, He is also a Holy God who hates sin. He is our creator and our judge. Being a just judge, He will make everyone pay for their sins. However, we will never be able to pay for our sins, ever!

In the book of Leviticus, God commanded the Israelites to offer up spotless lambs as a sacrifice for their sins. And in the book of Isaiah, we see a prophecy about Jesus as the coming "Suffering Servant" who would take on the sins of the world.

He was prophesied to be rejected and put to death, but his death would have great significance. Just as the Old Testament lambs were sacrificed to pay for the sins of God's people, Jesus sacrificed himself to pay for the sins of the whole world.

He died in our place, taking on the punishment that we deserve. And, because he was without sin, his death was enough to pay for all the sins of the world. So now, whoever believes in Jesus Christ, His death at the cross, and His resurrection, can be forgiven and have eternal life.

BOYS

BIBLE

DEVOTIONS

Day 10

Accepting the Gift of Salvation

"But to all who did receive Him, He gave them the right to be children of God, to those who believe in His name."
John 1:12, HCSB

Jesus came to Earth and died a painful death, the most painful and shameful death as a criminal. He did it because of His love for us. He paid for our sins and offered a gift that was already paid for.

However, this gift cannot be yours unless you admit that you need it. You have to believe that you are sinful and you need Jesus' sacrifice at the cross to be saved. You need to accept Jesus as your savior and the Lord of your life.

By doing this, you are putting your faith in Him. You trust that He paid for your sins and that He alone can save you by His grace. It is a decision that will change your life forever. If you have not accepted Jesus Christ as your Savior, I encourage you to do so today. He is waiting with open arms to welcome you into His kingdom.

If you're not sure what to do, you can also ask your Pastor or your Sunday School teacher to help you.

Once you make the decision to receive the gift of salvation, you will be born again. The Holy Spirit will make your heart His temple, and you be considered a child of God.

21

Repentance

"Repent, then, and turn to God, so that your sins may be wiped out, that times of refreshing may come from the Lord."
Acts 3:19, NIV

To turn your back to sin and face God, you first must realize that you are a sinner who needs repentance. To repent means to turn from sin and turn to God. It is acknowledging what we have been doing is wrong and choosing to change our ways. It is not just a one-time thing, but a continuous turning away from sin and turning towards God.

When we repent, we hate the sin that we have been living in and love the God we have been missing out on. We recognize our need for Him and His forgiveness.

Repentance is not easy, but it is worth it because it leads us back to the One who loves us and died for us. It is worth it because it brings healing to our hearts.

Once you have recognized your sinfulness, repentance means you're hating sin and loving God. It is not easy, but it is possible with the help of God's grace. If you are willing to repent and turn your life over to God, He will forgive you and give you the strength to live a life that is pleasing to Him.

BOYS

BIBLE

DEVOTIONS

New Life in Christ

*"Therefore, if anyone is in Christ, he is a new creation.
The old has passed away; behold, the new has come."*
2 Corinthians 5:17, ESV

The moment you accept Jesus as your Lord and Savior, you let God into your heart to direct your every step. You become a true Christian and you begin a wonderful journey with God.

As a true Christian, you are connected to God through the power of Jesus' blood. And as a Christian, you are also called to turn away from your sin and to follow Jesus.

This can be a difficult process because we can easily commit sin. But overcoming sins is essential for your spiritual growth.

When we become Christians, we become new creations. We are no longer bound by our sins. Instead, we are free to live a pure and holy life. This does not mean that we will never sin again, but it does mean that we have the power to overcome sin and follow Jesus.

When we turn our lives over to Christ, we find freedom from sin and a new purpose in life. We are no longer slaves to our sinful desires. Instead, we are free to serve God and love others.

If you are struggling with sin in your life, I encourage you to turn to Christ and ask him to give you the strength to overcome it. Christ died for our sins so that we could be forgiven and set free. He wants us to live lives that honor him, and he will help us if we only ask.

The Narrow Road

"Enter through the narrow gate. For wide is the gate and broad is the road that leads to destruction, and many enter through it. But small is the gate and narrow the road that leads to life, and only a few find it."
Matthew 7:13-14, NIV

As Christians, we are called to follow Jesus even when it's difficult. It can be easy to go with the flow, but Jesus calls us to a narrow road, which leads to life. The popular path may be broad and easy, but it ultimately leads to destruction.

When Jesus calls us to follow Him, we are called to step out in faith. This can be a difficult thing to do, especially when we are surrounded by people who make fun of Christians for their beliefs.

It can be easy to get caught up in what other people think of us and to start questioning our own faith. But if we fix our eyes on Jesus and strive to please Him only, He will give us the strength we need to stand firm in our faith.

When we keep our focus on Him, He will help us to ignore the criticisms of others and to live our lives for His glory. So let us continue to follow Him, even when the path is narrow and difficult, knowing that He will never lead us astray.

BOYS

BIBLE

DEVOTIONS

Day 14

Walking by Faith

"For we walk by faith, not by sight."
2 Corinthians 5:7, ESV

We live in a world that is constantly trying to tell us what to believe. Whether it's the media, our friends, or even our family, there are always voices trying to influence our perspectives. It can be difficult to know who to trust or what to think. As Christians, we are called to walk by faith, not by sight.

Many people think that faith means blindly believing in something without any proof. But that's not really what faith is. When Christians talk about faith, they mean trusting in God even when we can't see or understand what He is doing.

We live by faith because we believe that God is good and He has our best interests at heart. Does that mean that bad things will never happen to us? Of course not. But it does mean that we can trust God to work all things - the good and the bad - together for our good (Romans 8:28).

So, we should always put our trust in God, even when things around us might seem uncertain. We know that God is good and that His plan for us is perfect. Even when the path ahead is unclear, we can trust that He will guide our steps.

Day 15

His Faithful Promises

"If we are faithless, he remains faithful—
for he cannot deny himself."
2 Timothy 2:13, ESV

God's faithfulness is something that we can always rely on. He is a promise keeper and will always do what He says He will do.

God has promised us many things in the Bible, and He is faithful in keeping each of them. In Genesis, God promised to make Abraham the father of many nations. And in Exodus, He promised to deliver His people from slavery. Throughout the Old Testament, He promised to send a Messiah who would suffer and die for the sins of the world.

It wasn't easy for Jesus to live as a human being and to endure the torture that he had to go through. Yet, He chose death so that we can have a life with Him.

Moreover, God promised that those who believe in Jesus will be saved, and we can trust his word completely. When He assures us that He will never leave us or forsake us, we can rest assured that His presence will always be with us.

So when you're feeling lost and alone, remember that God is always with you. He loves you so much that He didn't even spare His own son for your sake. He will always do good to you. Just stay close to Him, obey His word, and trust him in everything.

BOYS

BIBLE

DEVOTIONS

PART 3

Overcoming Life's Challenges

Day 16

Conquering Your Fear

"Even though I walk through the darkest valley,
I will fear no evil, for you are with me; your
rod and your staff, they comfort me."
Psalm 23:4, NIV

King David, the man after God's own heart, was once a shepherd who took care of his father's sheep. When he wrote Psalm 23, he was going through a tough time and saw God as the greatest shepherd.

By comparing himself to a helpless sheep, he found comfort in knowing that the Lord is his Shepherd. He turned to God and put his trust in Him.

As a result, David was able to find strength and comfort in the Lord. And even today, just as a shepherd cares for his flock, God watches over us and protects us from harm. Like a good shepherd, He knows our every need and will never abandon us to fend for ourselves.

In His care, we are safe from all danger and can find true peace and contentment. We are never alone, even in our darkest moments. When we face our fears head-on, we can overcome them with the help of God. In doing so, we can emerge stronger and more resilient than before.

So if you're feeling afraid, remember that you are not alone. Take comfort in knowing that God is with you, and use His strength to conquer your fears.

BOYS

BIBLE

DEVOTIONS

Day 17

Managing Your Anger

"In your anger do not sin."
Ephesians 4:26, NIV

We've all felt anger at one time or another. Maybe someone cut you off in a line, or maybe you had a bad day at school. Whatever the reason, anger is a natural emotion. But sometimes, our anger can get the best of us. In Ephesians 4:26, we are instructed not to sin in our anger. In other words, it's okay to be angry, but we need to make sure that our anger doesn't lead us to sin. So how can we do that?

First, it's important to understand that anger is not always bad. It can also help us stand up for ourselves and others. But when our anger is out of control, it can lead to problems. That's why it's important to learn how to manage our anger in a healthy way.

One way to do this is by prayerfully considering the situation that made you angry. Ask God for wisdom and guidance on how to deal with the situation in a way that honors Him.

To do that, make sure you pray and give yourself some time to cool off before you respond to the situation that made you angry. This will help you avoid reacting in an unhealthy way. Learning how to manage your anger is an important step in living a godly life.

Day 18

Coping with Sorrow

"The LORD is close to the brokenhearted and saves those who are crushed in spirit."
Psalm 34:18, NIV

It's always tough when something bad happens. Maybe you've just had a bad day, or maybe it's been a string of bad days. Whatever the case may be, you need a pick-me-up from time to time. And thankfully, we have a God who is always there for us, no matter what.

When you're feeling sad, God will always stay close to you. He will never leave your side, and He will always help you through whatever it is that's got you down.

This doesn't mean that He will take away our hurt or magically make everything better. But it does mean that He will be with you in the midst of it. Sometimes, God allows us to experience pain for different reasons. Sometimes, it's to teach us a lesson or help us grow in our faith. Other times it's because He knows we need to lean on Him for strength and comfort.

So, if you are feeling sad or lost right now, know that God is right there with you. He sees your pain, He hears your cries, and He knows exactly how you feel. Cry out to Him and let Him comfort and sustain you in this difficult time. Don't be afraid to lean on Him during those tough times. He's always there for you, waiting with open arms.

BOYS

BIBLE

DEVOTIONS

Vanquishing Your Worry

"Therefore I tell you, do not worry about your life, what you will eat or drink; or about your body, what you will wear..."
Matthew 6:25a, NIV

People often worry about many things, and doing so usually causes a lot of stress. However, the Bible clearly teaches us to stop worrying. God knows that worrying does not help us or make us better people. Instead, it hinders our growth and prevents us from living productive lives.

Remember, God is in control of everything that happens in our lives. He has a plan for us, and He will work everything out for our good. Also, worrying does not change the outcome of any situation. It simply makes us feel anxious and stressed.

Jesus tells us in Matthew 6:25-34 not to worry about things like what we will eat or drink or about our clothes. He says that we should instead focus on God and His Kingdom.

This is great advice that can help us to live stress-free lives. When we worry about these things, we are really just worrying about ourselves and our own needs. But when we focus on God, we are reminded that He is in control and that He will provide for us.

This doesn't mean that we shouldn't take care of ourselves, but it does mean that we shouldn't let our worries consume us. If we can keep our focus on God and His Kingdom, we will be able to live more peaceful and productive lives.

Day 20

Healing from Guilt

"If we confess our sins, he is faithful and just and will forgive us our sins and purify us from all unrighteousness."
1 John 1:9, NIV

Have you ever done something you knew was wrong? How did you feel about it? When we sin, the Holy Spirit may show us that we are wrong, so we can come to God and turn away from that sin.

The Bible teaches us that when we confess our sins, God will forgive us. And you know what's more encouraging about this verse? He will also cleanse us from all unrighteousness. This means that when we ask for God's forgiveness, He promises to forgive us and make us clean again.

That's amazing news! But sometimes, even after we've asked for God's forgiveness, we can still feel guilty. That's because Satan likes to remind us of our past mistakes and try to convince us that we are unworthy of God's love.

But the good news is that we can resist Satan's lies by meditating on what the Bible says about our identity in Christ. When we believe what the Bible says about who we are in Christ, it will change the way we think about ourselves and help us overcome feelings of guilt.

So if you're struggling with guilt, don't give up! Keep reading your Bible and believe what it says about you. You are a child of God, and He loves you no matter what!

BOYS

BIBLE

DEVOTIONS

Overcoming Procrastination

*"Whatever you do, do it enthusiastically, as
something done for the Lord and not for men."*
Colossians 3:23, HCSB

We put off doing that one task until the last minute, telling ourselves that we'll get to it eventually. But why do we do this? Why do we procrastinate? There could be a lot of reasons. Maybe we're afraid of failure. Or maybe we're just lazy. Whatever the reason, procrastination is something that Christians should avoid.

The Bible has a lot to say about the importance of hard work and perseverance. In Colossians 3:23, we are told to work hard at whatever we do and that we should also do so cheerfully! This is because when we do our work, we don't just do this because someone required us to do it but because we are working for the Lord.

Today's verse reminds us that our work should be done as an offering to God, not simply to please others.

We are also told in 2 Thessalonians 3:10 that "if you don't work, you don't eat." This verse emphasizes the importance of taking action in our lives instead of simply sitting around and waiting for things to happen.

These verses remind us that procrastination is not an option if we want to live a life that is pleasing to God. Instead, we must take action and work hard towards our goals. When we do this, we can overcome procrastination and achieve great things for God's glory.

Day 22

Dealing with Jealousy

"A peaceful heart gives life to the body.
But jealousy rots the bones."
Proverbs 14:30, NIRV

Have you ever felt jealous of someone? Maybe it was a friend who got a new toy or a brother or sister who got to stay up later than you. Jealousy is a normal emotion that kids feel, but as Christians, we shouldn't let jealousy take over.

Jealousy usually happens when we compare ourselves to others. We might see someone who has something that we want and think, "That's not fair!"

It's important to remember that everyone is different and that God made us each special in our own way. Just because somebody has something you want doesn't mean that there's something wrong with you. The next time you start to feel jealous, here are some things you can do:

-Talk to God about it. He knows how you're feeling, and He wants to help.

-Think about all the things that are good about you. Make a list of all the things you like about yourself. Remember, there's only one YOU in this world!

-Talk to a grown-up about how you're feeling. They can help you talk through your feelings and figure out what to do next.

BOYS

BIBLE

DEVOTIONS

God's second greatest commandment is that we love others as ourselves. So, be happy for others, even if sometimes, you don't get what they have. In God's perfect time, you will receive your own blessings. Or, maybe, you already have them, but you simply don't notice them yet.

34

PART 4

Following Jesus

Day 23

Living a Life of Compassion

"So in everything, do to others what you would have them do to you, for this sums up the Law and the Prophets."
Matthew 7:12, NIV

Imagine that you are having a bad day. Now imagine that someone does something nice for you, like hold the door open or give you a compliment. It would probably make your day a little bit better, right?

Well, when you do something nice for someone else, you are making their day better too! When you're kind to others and treat them well, you are showing compassion.

Compassion is when we care about other people and try to help them, even if they're not related to us. We should always try to treat others the way we would want to be treated. This means being kind, patient, and understanding. It also means taking into consideration their feelings and needs.

As Christians, we should be like Jesus, who showed us what it's like to be kind and loving. No matter who someone is or what they've done, they deserve to be treated with compassion.

When we're compassionate, we are showing our love for others. We are also making the world a better place by setting an example of how we should all treat each other.

BOYS

BIBLE

DEVOTIONS

Day 24

Persevering Through Tough Times

"Consider it pure joy, my brothers and sisters, whenever you face trials of many kinds, because you know that the testing of your faith produces perseverance."
James 1:2-3, NIV

When things are going well, it's easy to be happy and grateful. But when things get tough, it can be hard to keep a positive attitude. That's why it's important to remember that, as Christians, we are called to persevere through hard times. This doesn't mean that we always have to be happy on the outside, but deep down, we should know that God is using these difficult times to make us stronger.

Today's verse tells us to be happy even when we experience problems in life. Even though tough times are never fun, they can actually be a good thing. They give us an opportunity to grow and become more mature.

Picture this: You are like gold that's just been mined. You see, when gold is first mined, it's impure. It contains other elements that need to be removed in order for it to be pure gold. And, to remove those impurities, the gold has to be heated to a very high temperature.

This is kind of like what happens when we go through tough times. The problems we experience act as a fire that burns away the impurities in our lives. As a result, we come out of tough times stronger and purer.

So, the next time you're going through a tough time, remember that you're like gold undergoing the process of purification. And, just like gold, you'll come out stronger and purer on the other side.

37

Day 25

Trusting God's Plans

"Trust in the Lord with all your heart and
lean not on your own understanding."
Proverbs 3:5, NIV

Do you trust your Dad? If your Dad tells you not to do something because it's dangerous, would you stay away from that thing without question? Or, would you try it out to see for yourself?

When you say you trust someone, there really is no need to confirm what they say. You trust that they know better than you, and that they will only want what's best for you. Sometimes, your parents may make mistakes.

You may discover things that could improve how they do things. If that happens, I'm sure they will be proud of you. But generally, they give you advice because they know that's the best thing to do.

As a child of God, He also tells you certain things that you should obey without questions. And unlike your human parents, God never makes mistakes. You can never improve God's ways because they are perfect. All you need to do is trust Him. Trust that He knows what He's doing and that He will always do what's best for you.

We may not always know what the future holds, but one thing we can always rely on is God's love for us. He knows what's best for us and will never lead us astray.

So next time you're feeling lost or uncertain, take a deep breath and remember to trust in God. He has a plan for you – even if you can't see it right now – and his love for you is constant and sure. So relax, and let God take the wheel. He's got this. And he's got you.

BOYS

BIBLE

DEVOTIONS

Developing Loyalty

"A friend loves at all times, and a brother
is born for a time of adversity."
Proverbs 17:17, NIV

If you've ever been in a situation where your friend stopped hanging out with you because you got in trouble, you know how hurtful it can be. It can feel like a betrayal, and it can leave you feeling isolated and alone.

The Bible teaches us to stick with our friends and family, especially when they need us most. This doesn't mean that you should put up with bad behavior from your friends, but it does mean that you should stick by them when they're going through a tough time.

It's important to be there for them. Showing your support can make a big difference in their life, even if it's just being someone to talk to.

Today's verse reminds us that true friends are always there for each other, even when times are tough. In addition, the book of Ecclesiastes also has some wise words on the subject of loyalty, stating that "two are better than one...for if they fall, one will lift up his companion. But woe to him who is alone when he falls and has not another to help him up!" (4:9-10).

These verses highlight the importance of being loyal to our family and friends, as they will be there to support us when we need them most.

Giving from the Heart

"Each person should do as he has decided in his heart—not reluctantly or out of necessity, for God loves a cheerful giver."
2 Corinthians 9:7, HCSB

Have you ever shared something with a friend? It feels good to give, doesn't it? But what if someone just forced you to share something? Doesn't it sometimes feel like you wish you didn't have to share?

When you feel that way, you are giving begrudgingly. The Bible teaches us to give from the heart. When we share something to a group, or to someone, we should be happy that we are able to help them. After all, when we're in need, we also want others to share with us.

As a kid, think about the things you can share with others. It doesn't have to be material things all the time. You can give different things—whether it's your time, energy, money, or attention.

Other ways to give generously include helping out in the house or doing something nice for someone without expecting anything in return. When you willingly and happily share your resources and energy with others, you are doing what Jesus wants you to do.

When you give from the heart, you might not even think about what you're doing. You just do it because it feels like the right thing to do. And that's the best kind of giving. It doesn't have to be a big gesture. Sometimes, the smallest things can mean the most.

BOYS

BIBLE

DEVOTIONS

Day 28

Valuing Honesty

"A lip of truth endures forever, but a tongue of deception lasts only a moment."
Proverbs 12:19, HCSB

When you make a mistake, it's usually best to just come clean and tell your parents the truth. They'll be more likely to understand and forgive you if you're honest with them. If you try to cover up what you did by lying, it will only make things worse. Your parents will be hurt and disappointed that you lied to them, and they'll be even angrier about what you did in the first place. But why is lying such a big deal?

Throughout the Bible, God tells us never to lie or cheat others. One reason is that lying goes against the nature of God. God is truth, and therefore He hates lies. The devil, on the other hand, is the master of lies. By telling lies, we are aligning ourselves with the devil and his ways.

In contrast, honesty is the foundation of any healthy relationship. If we can't be honest with others, we can't build trust. And without trust, our relationships will be shallow and superficial at best. Honesty also shows that we respect and value others enough to tell them the truth, even when it's not easy.

So, live honestly before God and others, knowing that it pleases Him and blesses His people.

41

Day 29

Being Grateful for Everything

*"Give thanks in everything, for this is
God's will for you in Christ Jesus."*
1 Thessalonians 5:18, HCSB

Have you ever had one of those days where everything seems to be going wrong? Maybe you lost your new toy, your gadget died, and you had a misunderstanding with your best friend.

It can be easy to get caught up in all your day-to-day troubles and forget about all of the good things in your life. But no matter how bad our day is, there is always something to be thankful for. Maybe it's a roof over our head, a bed to sleep in, or the fact that we woke up this morning.

The Bible reminds us to be thankful both for the good and the bad. Today's verse reminds us that even when things are tough, we can still find reasons to be grateful.

We may not have control over everything that happens to us, but we can choose how we respond to it. When we focus on being thankful, even for the little things, it helps us to see God's hand at work in our lives. And when we are grateful, God will delight in blessing us with even more good things.

So, when you're having a bad day, take a moment to reflect on all of the things you have to be thankful for. It might just turn your whole day around.

BOYS

BIBLE

DEVOTIONS

Day 30

Finding Freedom in Forgiveness

"And be kind and compassionate to one another, forgiving one another, just as God also forgave you in Christ."
Ephesians 4:32, HCSB

When someone hurts us, it's hard to forgive. We might even hold onto that hurt for a long time. But God says that it's important for us to forgive others, because when we do, he will forgive us too.

Forgiving doesn't mean that we forget what happened or that we're okay with what the other person did. It just means that we're ready to move on and let go of the hurt. It's not just about saying the words "I'm sorry."

When we forgive someone, we stop hating the person who wronged us. We also set our hearts free from all the anger and hurt. Forgiving someone can be really hard, especially if they hurt us a lot. But it's important to remember that forgiveness is for us, not them. It's about letting go of all the negative feelings so we can feel peace and freedom in our hearts again.

When we forgive, we set our hearts free from all the negativity and pain. Instead, we start to feel peace and freedom. So when someone does something to upset you, think about whether or not you want to forgive them. It might be the best thing for you in the long run.

Day 31

Being Responsible

"So then each of us will give an account of himself to God."
Romans 14:12, ESV

As a child who's almost a teen, you probably heard this so many times: Be more responsible. But sometimes, people's expectations can be vague that you might feel confused about what exactly you should be doing.

To help clarify what being responsible could mean for you, it simply means being accountable for what you do, and understanding the consequences of your choices. It's important to learn this early on, so that when you're an adult, you can make good decisions and be responsible for yourself.

The Bible helps us understand what it means to be responsible through stories. We see people making both good and bad choices, and facing either rewards or punishments as a result. This teaches us that we are responsible for our own actions.

We can't blame our mistakes on others; we have to take responsibility for ourselves. This is a hard but important lesson to learn. Someday, we will be facing our Creator and He won't let us put the blame for our sins on someone else.

In your everyday life, you can practice taking responsibility. For example, if you make a mess, clean it up. If you borrow something from someone, return it in the same condition (or better). If you break something, apologize and offer to fix it or pay for it.

Taking responsibility for your actions shows that you're growing up and becoming more capable. It's a sign of maturity that will serve you well throughout your life.

BOYS

BIBLE

DEVOTIONS

Day 32

Taking Courage

"Be strong and courageous; don't be terrified or afraid of them. For it is the Lord your God who goes with you; He will not leave you or forsake you."
Deuteronomy 31:6, HCSB

Have you ever been so afraid of something that you didn't want to try it? Maybe it was a big dog, or going down a tall slide. It's normal to feel fear sometimes. But sometimes, fear can stop us from doing what is right, or from pursuing something we're passionate about.

That's why it's important to be courageous. Courage doesn't mean the absence of fear. It means facing our fears and doing what is right, even when we're afraid. When we're courageous, we trust that God is with us, and that gives us the strength to keep going.

In the Old Testament, we see Moses leading the Israelites out of slavery in Egypt. In the New Testament, we see Jesus and his disciples boldly proclaiming the Good News of God's love.

Throughout Scripture, we see people taking a courageous stand against injustice and oppression.

These examples only show us that when we are faced with difficult choices, God gives us the courage to do what is right, even when it is hard. So whatever you may be facing today, know that you are not alone. God is with you, giving you the strength and courage you need to face whatever comes your way.

Day 33

Praying for Wisdom

"If any of you lacks wisdom, let him ask God, who gives generously to all without reproach, and it will be given him."
James 1:5, ESV

There's always a first time for everything: The first time you rode a bike, the first time you went to school, the first time you tried a new food. And sometimes, the first time can be pretty scary, like the first time you have to do something all by yourself, without anyone else to help you. That can be really tough. But you know what? God is always there with you, even when you don't know what to do. And He promised that if we ask for wisdom, He will give it to us.

The Bible encourages us to ask God for wisdom. Asking for God's Wisdom is acknowledging that He is the source of all knowledge and understanding. It also teaches us that wisdom is something to be sought after diligently. We see this in the story of Solomon, who asked for wisdom when he became king and was given great insight because of it.

When we pray for wisdom, we ask God to help us view the world through His eyes and make decisions based on His will, not our own. And while this can sometimes be difficult, it is always worth it in the end.

BOYS

BIBLE

DEVOTIONS

46

PART 5

Loving your family

Day 34

Honoring Your Parents

"Honor your father and your mother, that your days may be long in the land that the Lord your God is giving you."
Exodus 20:12, ESV

Different cultures have different ways of honoring their parents. In some cultures, children bow to their elders as a sign of respect. In others, children are expected to stay silent in the presence of their elders. But no matter how you show it, it is important that you hold your parents with high respect. More importantly, God commands all of us to honor our parents.

When we think about honoring our parents, we usually think about obeying them. And while obedience is very important, it's not the only way to show honor. We can also show honor by listening and by spending time with them. You can also show honor to your parents by respecting their wishes. This doesn't mean that you have to do everything they say without considering your feelings or opinion. Instead, you should give a lot of weight to their advice because they have knowledge and experience in life that you still lack. Most of all, they only want what's best for you.

Honoring your parents is important – both for them and for you. There are a lot of ways to show them that they matter to you and that you value their opinion. So take a moment today to think about how you can show honor to your parents in your words and actions.

BOYS

BIBLE

DEVOTIONS

Day 35

Obeying Your Parents

"Children, obey your parents in the Lord, for this is right."
Ephesians 6:1, ESV

Should children listen to their parents? The culture around us seems confused about this. Some families seem like the children are in charge. But the Bible says that children should obey their parents and that parents should make sure their children obey them.

Children need to obey their parents because the gospel demands it. It is best if children obey their parents "in the Lord." This means that they put their faith in Jesus and then, because of their personal relationship with him, they do what brings glory to his name.

The gospel assures you that you can joyfully obey your parents. You know God is working in your heart when you start obeying mom and dad.

Obeying parents means also obeying God. When you defy or disobey your mom and dad, it would also be easy for you to disobey God. And that disobedience can ruin your life.

On the other hand, if you develop the discipline of obedience, it can be a way of learning to submit to God's will. Of course, there may be times when obeying our parents is not easy. But even when it is hard, remember that it is usually for your own good. After all, they are the ones who know you best and want what is best for you.

49

Day 36

Trusting Your Parents

"Train up a child in the way he should go, and even when he is old he will not depart from it."
Proverbs 22:6, ASV

Parents are usually the first people we learn to trust. They have taken care of us since we were helpless, little babies. And even though they might not be perfect, they're always there for us. That's why it's important to trust your parents, even when you grow up and start making your own decisions.

They've been through a lot in their lives. They've made mistakes and learned from them, so they're in a good position to help you avoid making the same mistakes.

In addition, they're also commanded by God to make sure they do their part in training you to become a man who fears and loves the Lord. So, no matter what, your parents want what's best for you. Even when they make you do things that you don't want to do, it's because they think it will ultimately benefit you in some way.

So, even if you don't understand why they're making you do something, trust that they have your best interests at heart. Even when you don't agree with them, or you think they're being too strict, remember that they're only trying to help you. And in the end, you'll be glad you listened to their advice.

BOYS

BIBLE

DEVOTIONS

Day 37

Caring for Your Siblings

"Be kind and compassionate to one another, forgiving each other, just as in Christ God forgave you."
Ephesians 4:32, NIV

If you have brothers or sisters, rejoice! The Bible tells us that siblings can influence us for our good. In fact, the relationships between siblings are unique and a gift from God.

Your siblings know you better than anyone else. They're the friends you didn't choose yourself. Yet, you accept each other's strengths and weaknesses. There are times when you may have little fights. Yet they love you anyway. That's a pretty good representation of God's unconditional love for us!

To top it all, your siblings make your life fun. From playing games to just hanging out and talking, spending time with our siblings can be a blast. And it's even more fun when you know we're doing it all for the glory of God!

Siblings are truly a gift from God. Not only can they teach us about His love, but they can also help us grow in our faith and provide companionship along the way.

So if you have siblings, cherish them! And if you don't have any biological siblings, don't worry—you probably have a friend or two who feels like a brother or sister to you anyway.

Day 38

Valuing Your Family

"Therefore, as we have opportunity, we must work for the good of all, especially for those who belong to the household of faith."
Galatians 6:10, HCSB

Families are the people who will always be there for us, no matter what. They are the people who know us best and love us anyway.

Families are important because they provide us with a support system. They are the people we can rely on when we need help or just someone to talk to. But sometimes, we may have disagreements with our family members.

It's okay to have different opinions from the people in our families. We're all entitled to our own thoughts and feelings. However, it's important to remember that we should always try to show our families love. Just because we disagree with them doesn't mean that we don't still care about them.

God wants us to love each other, even when it's hard. He knows that families can be tricky sometimes, but He also knows how important they are to us. We should always seek to be good to our parents and our siblings. And, we should love our grandparents and other members of the extended family.

When we love each other, even through tough times, it shows that we really do care about one another. Families are a gift from God, and He wants us to cherish them always.

BOYS

BIBLE

DEVOTIONS

PART 6

Cultivating Friendships

The Value of Friendship

*"The heartfelt counsel of a friend is as
sweet as perfume and incense."*
Proverbs 27:9, NLT

Can you imagine your life without friends? It would be awfully quiet, boring, and sad. That's because friendship is one of the best things in life.

Friends can help you when you're feeling down. They can make you laugh and help take your mind off things that are bothering you. Friends can also help you learn new things. If you're stuck on a project or don't understand something, your friends can help give you ideas or explain them to you in a way that makes sense.

Plus, friends are just fun to be around! But perhaps the most important reason why God wants us to have friendships is that they help us to see the world from another person's eyes. Through our friends, we learn about different views in life. We learn to appreciate the things that make us unique and to celebrate our commonalities. In short, friendships help us to become more compassionate and understanding people.

Sometimes, though, you may have little fights with your friends. They may say something that hurts you and you may have given them a smart answer. But that's okay. What's important is that they're able to work it out and remain friends. That's what makes friendship so special. They can make even the simplest activities more enjoyable. So go out there and make some friends!

BOYS

BIBLE

DEVOTIONS

Day 40

Jesus is Your Best Friend

*"Greater love has no one than this, that
someone lay down his life for his friends."*
John 15:13, ESV

If you are looking for a best friend who will always be there for you, look no further than Jesus Christ. Jesus is the best friend you will ever have!

One of the best things about Jesus is that He loves you no matter what. It doesn't matter if you make good grades or not, if you are popular or not, if you are athletic or not.

Jesus loves you just the way you are. That is something that no other friend can say.

Jesus is always there for you, whether you need someone to talk to in the middle of the night or someone to help you through a tough day. All you need to do is pray and He will listen. Jesus also forgives you no matter what.

If you make a mistake, all you need to do is ask for forgiveness and He will forgive you. This is something that no other friend can do. But most of all, Jesus died for you. He suffered unimaginable suffering to save you from your sins. No one will ever love you more than Jesus. With His unconditional love, His constant presence, and His willingness to forgive, Jesus makes the perfect best friend.

Day 41

Marks of a True Friend

"A man of many companions may come to ruin, but there is a friend who sticks closer than a brother."
Proverbs 18:24, ESV

We all have friends. But what makes a true friend? According to the Bible, it is possible for us to have many companions, or people we hang out with. But a true friend is someone who sticks by you, even when times are tough.

Today's verse tells us that it's better to have one or two close friends than a whole bunch of friends who don't really care for you. Sometimes, it's tempting to try to be friends with everyone. But it's better to have fewer friends who are really close to you than a lot of friends who don't really know you at all.

Also, a true friend isn't afraid to tell you the truth - even when it's something you don't want to hear. They would rather hurt your feelings by telling you the truth than see you make a mistake because they were too afraid to speak up.

Finally, just like what Jesus showed us through his friendship with his disciples, a true friend wants what's good for you. That's because they care about you. They won't push you to do bad things and get you in trouble. Instead, they try to stop you when you're doing something dangerous or bad.

BOYS
BIBLE
DEVOTIONS

Day 42

Learning to Say No

"Do not be deceived: Bad company ruins good morals."
1 Corinthians 15:33 ESV

It can be really hard to say no sometimes. Maybe your friends are doing something that you know you shouldn't do. It can be tempting to just go along with what everyone else is doing. But it's important to remember that you always have a choice.

Remember the story of Daniel and his three friends, Shadrach, Meshach, and Abednego. When everyone was enjoying food offered to idols, they chose to refuse the offer of delicious food. They choose to stand up for what they believe in, even when it's not popular.

Other people may laugh at you or maybe stop hanging out with you. Maybe they would think you're not cool. But God's opinion of you is all that matters.

God wants you to keep His word in your heart and to follow Jesus no matter what. You don't always have to talk back to defend your stand. Just know that you are responsible for your actions. At the end of the day, you cannot put the blame on your friends who encouraged you to do bad things. Whatever you decide to do is your responsibility, and you will face its consequences.

When you say no to things that aren't good for you, you're setting a good example for others by showing them that it's okay to stand up for what they believe in too. So next time someone offers you something that you know you shouldn't have, just say no!

How to Make a New Friend

"He has shown you, O mortal, what is good. And what does the Lord require of you? To act justly and to love mercy and to walk humbly with your God."
Mark 6:8, NIV

If there's a Bible verse that obviously tells you how to live your life, it is this verse. This should also be our guide when we're interacting with other people, especially when we are with people we don't know yet. So, what can we learn from this verse when making new friends?

First, be merciful and try to understand what other people may be feeling. Do not judge anyone based on their outward appearance. In short, do not judge people so easily. So, when you are with other people, don't just talk to the ones who you think would be nice to talk to. Try to notice everyone, especially the ones you may have ignored in the past.

Talk to people you don't know. Talk to people in your class, at your after-school activities, or even just people you see around your neighborhood. If you're shy, remember that they may be shy too. They may just be waiting for someone to start the conversation.

Let them feel that you are interested in knowing them. Ask them questions about themselves. It might make them feel comfortable and it will help you get to know them better. Finally, be humble. Don't try to impress others. Just be yourself, and the right people will like you for who you are.

BOYS

BIBLE

DEVOTIONS

Isolation

"For I am sure that neither death nor life, nor angels nor rulers, nor things present nor things to come, nor powers, nor height nor depth, nor anything else in all creation, will be able to separate us from the love of God in Christ Jesus our Lord."
Romans 8:38-39, ESV

There are times when we all feel isolated and alone. Maybe you're the new kid at school and you don't know anyone. Or maybe you're going through a tough time and all your friends seem to be busy.

Whatever the reason, isolation can be a really tough feeling. But there's a comfort to be found in knowing that even Jesus felt isolated at times. But no matter what, God is with us and nothing can separate us from Him.

Jesus was betrayed by one of his close friends, Judas, and then denied by another friend, Peter.

Can you imagine how alone and isolated Jesus must have felt at that moment? But even though he was alone, he still had a relationship with God. He knew that God was with him, even in his darkest hour.

The Bible teaches us that isolation is a part of life but we can still have a relationship with God even when we're feeling alone. So if you're ever feeling isolated or alone, remember that you're not alone in your feelings and that God is always with you.

Being a Good Friend

*"Everyone should look out not only for his own
interests, but also for the interests of others."*
Philippians 2:4, HCSB

Friendship is a two-way street. It's not just about receiving; it's also about giving. A good friend is someone who is there for you when you need them, and someone you can count on to be a shoulder to cry on. But being a good friend isn't always easy.

In the Bible story of Jonathan and David, we see how two friends can stick together even when their families are fighting. Jonathan's father, King Saul, was jealous of David and wanted to kill him. But Jonathan stuck by his friend anyway. He warned David that his father was looking for him, and he even gave him his own sword and armor to protect him. Jonathan knew that it wasn't right for his father to treat David like that, and he was willing to risk everything to help his friend. That's what a good friend does.

When you see someone being treated unfairly, you stand up for them even if it means getting into trouble yourself. That's what Jonathan did, and that's what we should all aspire to do.

If you're looking for some guidance on how to be a good friend, learn from Jonathan. He was looking out for David and did his best to help him. He was simply there when his friend needed him most.

BOYS

BIBLE

DEVOTIONS

Day 46

Active Listening

"My dearly loved brothers, understand this: Everyone must be quick to hear, slow to speak, and slow to anger."
James 1:19, HCSB

Have you ever been in a conversation with someone and they seemed like they were barely listening to what you were saying? Maybe they were looking around the room, or their mind seemed to be somewhere else entirely. Sometimes, they may also be quick to speak, without hearing what you have to say first. It can be really frustrating!

On the other hand, have you ever talked to someone who was hanging on your every word? These conversations are usually a lot more enjoyable. So, how can you become a better listener? As the Bible says, we should spend more time listening to others instead of always trying to talk.

So, the first thing to remember when listening to a friend is to let the person finish what he or she is saying before you start talking. Not only is it rude to interrupt, but it also shows that you weren't really listening in the first place. You can also encourage your friend to share his or her thoughts by looking at their eyes. It's a sign that you're interested in what they have to say. Finally, make sure you ask your friend some questions.

Active listening is a skill that takes practice, but it›s worth it because it can make conversations more meaningful and enjoyable!

Day 47

Taking Sides

"My dear friends, as a follower of our Lord Jesus Christ, I beg you to get along with each other. Don't take sides. Always try to agree in what you think."
1 Corinthians 1:10, CEV

It's easy to choose sides. In fact, it's probably one of the first things we learn to do as kids. We choose our favorite color, our favorite animal, and our favorite sports team. And pretty soon, we learn to choose sides in more important matters, like politics and religion. But why does the Bible tell us not to take sides?

When you choose a side, you're usually doing so based on the information you have at the time. But what if you don't have all the information? What if there are facts that you don't know about that would change your opinion? It's important to be open-minded and consider all the facts before making a decision about which side to take.

Sometimes there isn't a right or wrong answer. There are just different opinions. In these cases, it's okay to agree to disagree. You don't have to take sides just for the sake of taking sides. It's perfectly fine to have your own opinion and not worry about what everyone else thinks. Instead, you should always care about the truth.

People may make mistakes, even the ones you love the most. So, in conflicts, always stop yourself from taking sides too quickly and let your friends or family explain their side of the story.

BOYS

BIBLE

DEVOTIONS

Day 48

Encouraging a Friend

*"Therefore encourage one another and build
each other up as you are already doing."*
1 Thessalonians 5:11, HCSB

Being a good friend is important, but it's not always easy. Think about it this way: when you're feeling down, who do you want by your side? Someone who makes you feel worse, or someone who makes you feel better? We all want friends who will lift us up when we're feeling low. That's what it means to encourage your friends.

Sometimes, your friends may just need someone to lend a listening ear. When they're going through a tough time, just being there for them can make all the difference. So the next time your friend comes to you with a problem, resist the urge to give advice and just listen instead. Let them know that you care and that you're there for them no matter what.

More importantly, pray for your friends. Pray that God would give them strength in their time of need, that He would bless them abundantly, and that they would know His love more deeply than ever before.

Finally, tell your friends the truth. If your friend is headed down a path that you know is harmful, have the courage to speak up and tell them the truth—in love. Help them see things from a different perspective and encourage them to make wise choices.

Day 49

Dealing with Conflict

"A gentle answer turns away wrath,
but a harsh word stirs up anger."
Proverbs 15:1, NIV

Let's face it, conflict is a part of life. Whether you're arguing with your siblings, your friends, or even your parents, it's bound to happen from time to time. But what does the Bible have to say about how we should deal with conflict?

Today's verse is a great reminder that our words have power. When we're in the midst of an argument, it's easy to let our emotions get the best of us and say things that we don't really mean. But if we can take a step back and respond in a calm and collected manner, chances are the other person will do the same.

Another important thing to remember is to apologize when we're in the wrong. When we hold onto our pride and refuse to admit that we're wrong, it only makes the situation worse. On the other hand, when we're willing to humble ourselves and admit that we made a mistake, it can go a long way in diffusing the situation.

But what if, after thinking it through calmly, we realize that they're really wrong? Well, it's really okay to be upset. But we should never allow our anger to turn into hatred or bitterness.

If we can learn to deal with our conflict in a healthy way—not letting our emotions get the best of us— then chances are good that the situation will be resolved quickly and without any lasting damage.

BOYS

BIBLE

DEVOTIONS

Day 50

Praying for Others

*"Therefore confess your sins to each other and pray
for each other so that you may be healed. The prayer
of a righteous person is powerful and effective."*
James 5:16, NIV

Prayer is an important part of the Christian faith. When we pray, we talk to God and ask for His help. But did you know that it's also important to pray for other people?

When you pray for your friends, you may not see the results right away. But that doesn't mean that God isn't listening. In fact, your prayers can have a powerful impact on their lives, even if you don't know it.

When you pray for your friends, you are asking God to bless them, protect them, and give them strength. You are also asking God to work in their lives in ways that only He can. So don't be discouraged if you don't see an immediate change in your friend's life. Just know that when you pray for them, you are unleashing the power of prayer on their behalf.

One of the most important things we can do as Christians is to love others. And one way we can show our love is by praying for them.

When you take the time to pray for someone, it shows them that you care about them and that you are thinking of them. It's a simple way to let someone know that you are there for them.

PART 7

Being a Christian at School

Day 51

Respecting Teachers

"Let everyone be subject to the governing authorities, for there is no authority except that which God has established. The authorities that exist have been established by God."
Romans 13:1, NIV

Have you ever talked back to a grown-up and he or she thought you were being disrespectful? Sometimes, you may sound disrespectful even though all you want is to explain your point. No matter our opinion, the Bible tells us we should respect those in positions of authority because they are there for a reason.

God has put them there to help us and guide us. We should pray for them and be thankful for them.

Teachers are some of the most important people in our lives. They have a big job to do! They help us learn new things, grow as people, and reach our goals.

So it's important that we show them the respect they deserve. That doesn't mean we always have to agree with them or do what they say, but it does mean listening to them and being polite. It also means being appreciative when they go above and beyond for us. A little respect can go a long way in making sure our teachers always have our backs.

When we respect those who are there to help us, we are showing God that we are grateful for His guidance. So next time you're tempted to roll your eyes or talk back to your teacher, remember what they deserve instead love and respect.

Day 52

Treating Everyone with Kindness

*"So in everything, do to others what you would have them
do to you, for this sums up the Law and the Prophets."*
Matthew 7:12, NIV

If you're unsure how to act in a certain situation, just think: How would I like other people to treat me if I were in his/her shoes? The verse above, also called the Golden Rule, is one basic thing we all have to embrace to make sure we all live in kindness with each other.

If we treat others the way we want to be treated, it can go a long way in making sure that everyone feels respected and valued.

Not only should we treat others with kindness, but we should also do what is best for them. We should think about what would be best for someone else and then do that. When we truly care for other people's good, we show the love that Jesus wants us to have for the world.

Remember, Jesus loves everyone so much, He died on the cross to pay for each person's sins. So, we should love everybody too. If Jesus, who is pure and perfect, loves them, then who are we to look down on them? Yes, we are all created unique from each other, but we are loved by God. And, God desires that we love each other too.

BOYS

BIBLE

DEVOTIONS

Day 53

Bullying in School

*"Anyone who claims to be in the light but hates
a brother or sister is still in the darkness."*
1 John 2:9, NIV

It's no secret that bullying is a big problem. Every day, kids go to school feeling scared and alone, wondering if they're going to be the next victim of some mean kid's torment. The Bible teaches us that it's wrong to mistreat those who are weaker than us.

God created each of us for a specific purpose, and we should respect His creation by not mistreating those who are weaker than us. This includes picking on someone who is smaller or younger than us, or making fun of someone because they don't have as much money or possessions as we do.

But what if you're one who gets bullied?

When you're the victim of bullying, you might be afraid to tell your parents or teachers, or you might feel like you can handle it on your own. But it's important to remember that you're not alone. Here are some things you can do if you're being bullied:

-Talk to someone you trust, like a parent, teacher, or pastor. They can help you figure out what to do next.

-Pray for strength and wisdom. God will give you the courage and guidance you need to face this challenge.

Remember that God loves you and has a plan for your life. No matter what others say or do, know that you are valuable and loved.

Expressing Yourself

*"And whatever you do, whether in word or deed,
do it all in the name of the Lord Jesus, giving
thanks to God the Father through him."*
Colossians 3:17, NIV

We all have different ways of expressing ourselves. Some people like to express themselves through art, music, or writing. Others express themselves through their fashion choices, the way they style their hair, or the tattoos they have. No matter how you choose to express yourself, it's important to do it in a way that is respectful and positive.

In today's verse, it is obvious that expressing ourselves doesn't just deal with our clothing choices. But it is a good reminder that the way we treat others should be an expression of our love for them. It's also important to remember that our words and actions can be expressions of who we are on the inside.

In addition, Ephesians 4:29 says "Do not let any unwholesome talk come out of your mouths, but only what is helpful for building others up according to their needs, that it may benefit those who listen."

This verse is a good reminder that our words should build others up, not tear them down. So, no matter how upset we may be, we should remember to pause and weigh our words and actions first before we do or say something hurtful.

BOYS

BIBLE

DEVOTIONS

Day 55

Developing Good Habits

"Do not be conformed to this world, but be transformed by the renewal of your mind, that by testing you may discern what is the will of God, what is good and acceptable and perfect."
Romans 12:2, ESV

A lot of things in the world can try to pull you down or make you act in a way that isn't true to who you are. It's important to resist those things - to stand up for what you believe in, even when it's hard.

One way to do that is by making sure that your mind is clear and thinking about what the right thing to do is. That way, when something happens, you'll already have a plan for how to deal with it. You'll know what God wants you to do, and you can act on that.

And how do you develop that skill? Young as you are, it's never too early to develop good habits. If you develop good habits, like praying and reading the Bible, you will grow up into a man who loves and serves God and His kingdom.

Also, good habits will help you grow in holiness. Holiness is living in a way that is pleasing to God. It's living according to His standards, not the world's standards.

Developing good habits will train your heart and mind to think and act in a way that is pleasing to God. The more you do something, the easier it becomes. So if you want to live holy lives, we need to develop habits that will help us to do that.

Day 56

Valuing Education

*"Whatever you do, work heartily,
as for the Lord and not unto men."*
Colossians 3:23, ESV

Many people believe that getting an education is important so you can have the knowledge and skills for your future. They are not wrong, but there is more to it than that. Getting an education is important for yourself, your parents, your community, and most of all, for God.

If you value your education, it shows that you value the life that God has given you. It shows that you are willing to do your best and put in the effort to learn as much as you can. When you do your best at school, it not only benefits you, but it also benefits your parents and your community.

Remember, your parents want you to get an education so you can have a better future. They want you to be able to support yourself someday. Most of all, though, getting an education is important for God.

He wants you to use the talents and gifts He has given you. He wants you to do your best and to be the best you can be. Getting an education is one way you can show Him that you are grateful for what He has done for you.

So, study hard and always do your best, not just to get a good grade or even a good future. But do your best as your personal offering to God.

BOYS

BIBLE

DEVOTIONS

Day 57

God and Science

"He spreads out the northern skies over empty space; he suspends the earth over nothing."
Job 26:7, NIV

Who would have thought that the Bible, written thousands of years ago, would contain information that is only now being confirmed by modern science?

Today's verse is an excellent example of how the Bible can provide guidance and wisdom beyond our current understanding. In this case, the Bible tells us that the earth is round and floats in space—two facts that were not discovered by explorers and scientists until relatively recently.

It's no secret that people think God cannot be combined with science. In school, we're taught that God didn't create the universe and that He isn't real. Some might say that science has disproved the existence of God, but that simply isn't true. In fact, many scientists believe in God because they have seen firsthand how His handiwork is evident in all aspects of our world. From the smallest particle to the largest galaxy, everything points to a Creator who is infinitely smarter and more powerful than we could ever imagine.

When we look closely at science, it's clear that God is a part of it. So next time you're being bombarded with information about how godless science is, don't believe it! Instead, remember that it was all created by the one true Creator—God Himself.

Day 58

Handling Embarrassment

"Fools show their annoyance at once,
but the prudent overlook an insult."
Proverbs 12:16, NIV

Let's face it, we've all been there. You're riding the school bus and realized you were wearing house slippers, or your little brother told everyone you had a crush on some girl. We've all been there, and it's not fun. But the Bible teaches us to not be so annoyed by things. Instead, it would be wise to overlook an insult. This means that it's better to just ignore an embarrassing moment and move on instead of dwelling on it and getting upset.

Also, when you're embarrassed, try to remember these tips:

1. Pray for guidance. Ask God to help you handle the situation with grace and dignity.

2. Keep your sense of humor. Don't take things too seriously and laugh it out.

3. Apologize if necessary. A sincere apology can go a long way in diffusing the situation and making things right again.

4. Move on quickly. Once you've dealt with the situation as best you can, it's important to move on quickly.

Don't dwell on the embarrassment; just let it go and move on with your day. Others may still remember your embarrassing moment after a few hours or days. But if you don't take it seriously, chances are they will also forget about it easily.

BOYS

BIBLE

DEVOTIONS

Day 59

Cheating is Never an Option

*"Truthful words stand the test of time,
but lies are soon exposed."*
Proverbs 12:19, NLT

It's not uncommon for kids to lie or cheat in school. Whether it's because they don't want to get in trouble or they're just trying to get a better grade, it happens. And if you're caught, it can be really embarrassing. But as a Christian, you should never cheat, not because it's scary to be caught, but because it is a sin against God. Cheating goes against everything we believe in and it dishonors God.

When we cheat, we are essentially telling God that we don't think He is enough. We don't trust that He will help us get the grades we need without resorting to dishonest means. Cheating also puts us at risk of being caught and facing serious consequences.

In addition, cheating gives you a false sense of accomplishment. You might get a good grade on the test, but you didn't really learn anything. In the long run, that's not going to help you.

The next time you're tempted to cheat, remember that it's not worth the risk. There's no honor in cheating and it's not what God wants for us. We need to trust Him to help us succeed and be honest in all that we do.

Day 60

Finding Your Interests

"Based on the gift each one has received, use it to serve others, as good managers of the varied grace of God."
1 Peter 4:10, HCSB

God gave us unique gifts for a purpose. But how can you serve Him with these gifts if you don't know what they are? To find your purpose in life, you must first find your interests. Once you know the things you are passionate about, it becomes much easier to see how your talents and abilities can be put to good use.

Some people, they get to discover and develop their talents early in life. But for others, it is not so easy. If you don't know what your interests are yet, think about the things that you have enjoyed doing in the past. What are the things that you have always been drawn to? What are the things that make you lose track of time because you enjoy them so much?

These are all clues as to what your interests might be. Another way to find your interests is to think about the things that you are good at. What are the things that come easily to you? What are the things that you get compliments on from other people? These are also clues as to what your interests might be.

Once you have a list of potential interests, you start exploring them. That way, you can hone your skills and use them to serve God.

BOYS

BIBLE

DEVOTIONS

Day 61

Setting Goals

"Commit to the LORD whatever you do,
and he will establish your plans."
Proverbs 16:3, NIV

You have your whole life ahead of you and you may have so many dreams and plans for your life. Do you want to be a doctor, an astronaut, or a professional athlete? You might not know how you're going to achieve your dreams. But have faith that anything is possible. The key to making our dreams come true is to involve God in the process.

The first step to involving God in your plans is prayer. Talk to God about what you want to do with your life. He already knows your heart's desire, but it's important for you to communicate with Him about it. Prayer is a two-way conversation, so don't just talk at Him; listen for His guidance too.

Another way to involve God in your plans is by reading His Word, the Bible. Scripture is full of stories of people who followed God's will for their lives, even when it wasn't easy. As you read these stories, ask God to show you how He wants you to live your life.

Whatever your dreams are, make God a part of your plan. Stay focused on His will for your life and He'll guide you along the way.

Day 62

Adopting a Growth Mindset

"He gives power to the faint, and to him who has no might he increases strength."
Isaiah 40:29, ESV

Have you ever tried learning something new? When you try doing something for the first time, it's normal to find it extra challenging. But when you don't give up and keep trying, you will eventually learn that new skill. And if you believe that you can grow and improve with effort, you have a "growth mindset."

Having a growth mindset means that you don't easily give up. As a Christian, you definitely should adopt a growth mindset because you have a God who strengthens you. And even when you feel weak, you can trust that God will turn your weaknesses into strengths. If you have a growth mindset, you'll never give up because you know that there's always room for improvement. No matter how hard something is, you'll keep trying because you believe that you can get better with practice.

In addition, adopting a growth mindset means that you learn from your mistakes instead of getting discouraged by them. You know that making mistakes is part of the learning process and that every mistake is an opportunity to grow and improve.

Remember, if you believe that God gives you power, He will turn your weaknesses into strengths. He has big plans for your life—plans to use your unique gifts and talents to bless others and make the world a better place. So don't give up—keep reaching for the stars!

BOYS

BIBLE

DEVOTIONS

Be an Example

"Let no one despise your youth; instead, you should be an example to the believers in speech, in conduct, in love, in faith, in purity."
1 Timothy 4:12, HCSB

As a young Christian, God wants you to set a good example for those around you! Whether you're at school, at home, or out with your friends, people are always watching and learning from what you do. So, be an example in your speech. No matter who you're talking to, always use kind words. You never know what somebody is going through, and even just a few kind words can really brighten somebody's day.

You should also be an example in action. If you see somebody who looks like they could use some help, offer to help them! It could be carrying something heavy for them or even just holding the door open. Little things can make such a big difference, and people will definitely remember your act of kindness. Also, be honest in everything you do. People will respect you more if they know they can trust you.

Sometimes, your friends may encourage you to speak bad things about other kids. Or, maybe the media shows you that it's ok to be disrespectful. But remember, as a young Christian, you have the opportunity to set a great example for those around you!

When you become more careful about what you say or do for Jesus's sake, you're showing everyone the love that Jesus has for everyone. You're encouraging them to be followers of Jesus too.

PART 8

More than Just a Game

Day 64

Team Spirit

"And all who believed were together and had all things in common. And they were selling their possessions and belongings and distributing the proceeds to all, as any had need."
Acts 2:44-45, ESV

Have you ever played on a sports team, or been part of a group project at school? If so, then you know what it means to be a team player. Being a team player is important because it helps you learn how to work well with others.

In the book of Acts, early Christians grew as a church by working together for the good of everyone in the church. When you work as part of a team, you're practicing one of the values that God wants us to develop: Teamwork.

When you try your best as a member of a group or a team, you can help figure out ways to achieve your common goals. This can be challenging at times, but it's also a lot of fun! And it's a skill that will come in handy later in life.

When you're part of a team, you need to be able to communicate effectively with your teammates. This means learning how to listen carefully and express yourself clearly.

Working as part of a team can help you develop these important communication skills. There will be times when you don't agree with your teammates on everything.

That's okay! What's important is that you learn how to find solutions that everyone can agree on. You also have to cooperate with others. This means working together towards a common goal and pitching in when someone needs help.

81

God's Victory

"But thanks be to God, who gives us the victory through our Lord Jesus Christ."
1 Corinthians 15:57, NASB

Everyone loves to win, whether it's in a sports game, a board game, or just in life in general. It feels good to know that you're better than someone else at something. But it's important to remember that every good thing comes from God. He is the one who gives you victory.

So, when you win, be a good winner and thank God. Be humble in your victory. This doesn't mean you can't be happy about winning—you totally should be! But don't let your happiness turn into arrogance.

Be thankful and remember that it was given to you by God. So, resist the urge to gloat. No one likes a show-off. So even if you are feeling really good about your win, resist the urge to rub it in the other person's face. Instead, congratulate the other person graciously.

Even though they didn't come out on top this time, they are still deserving of your congratulations. Take the time to shake their hand or give them a hug and tell them congratulations on a job well done—even if that job didn't result in a win for them this time around.

Winning feels great, but it's important to remember that God is the one who gives us victory. So when you do win, don't forget to thank Him and be a humble winner.

BOYS

BIBLE

DEVOTIONS

Day 66

Respecting the Opponents

"Do nothing out of rivalry or conceit, but in humility consider others as more important than yourselves."
Philippians 2:3, HCSB

When you play a team game, how do you feel about the other team? While you want to win a game, and wish the other team to lose, it's important to show good sportsmanship.

Sportsmanship is when you show respect for your opponents and play fair. It's also about being a good winner or loser. And, whether they win or lose against you, God wants you to be humble and not treat others with rivalry.

Everyone deserves to be treated with dignity and respect, no matter who they are or what they have done. So, you should not be arrogant when you win.

You can still be happy and excited about your win, but don't do it at the expense of the other person's feelings. Just because you won doesn't mean the other person didn't try hard. In fact, they probably tried just as hard as you did—they just didn't happen to come out on top this time. So, take a moment to acknowledge their effort and tell them that you respect them as an opponent.

Respecting others shows that you are confident in yourself and your own abilities.

You don't need to put others down in order to feel good about yourself. Also, respecting others will help you build strong relationships with the people around you. When you build strong relationships with others, you get the opportunity to share God's love with them.

Day 67

Be Gracious to Your Teammates

"Make allowance for each other's faults, and forgive anyone who offends you. Remember, the Lord forgave you, so you must forgive others."
Colossians 3:13, NLT

When you're losing in a game, it's easy to get caught up in the heat of the moment and blame your teammates when things go wrong. But as a Christian, you are called to a higher standard. You are called to be gracious and forgiving, especially when others make mistakes.

When your team makes a mistake, it can be tempting to point the finger and lay the blame squarely at their feet. They are probably just as upset about the loss as you are. Yelling at them or calling them names will not make the situation better. Instead, try to be understanding and offer encouragement. Let them know that you are still on their side and that you will work together to improve for the next game. Blaming them does not solve the problem, but creates division within your team. And when you're divided, you're more likely to lose.

So, when they make a mistake, take a deep breath and remember that they are human just like you. Everyone makes mistakes, and you need to be patient with them. Talk to them about what happened. Listen to their side of the story and help them see how their mistake might have impacted the team. Finally, forgive them. Just as God has forgiven you, we need to forgive your teammates for their mistakes.

BOYS

BIBLE

DEVOTIONS

84

Day 68

Facing Defeats

*"We are pressured in every way but not crushed;
we are perplexed but not in despair."*
2 Corinthians 4:8, HCSB

We all want to win. Whether it's in a game, in a competition, or in life itself, we always strive to be victorious. And while winning is great, it's important to remember that losing is a part of life too. In fact, losing can be just as important as winning, if not more so.

Losing can teach us some important lessons that we might not otherwise learn. For example, losses can teach us how to be humble. They can also show us that we need to work harder if we want to achieve our goals.

Of course, it's important to remember that not all defeats are created equal. Some losses are more significant than others, and it's perfectly natural to feel upset after experiencing a major setback. However, it's important to pick yourself up and keep going.

The Bible reminds us that even when we feel so much pressure, we are never really crushed. Defeats don't mean there's no more hope for us. Because we have a good Father in Heaven, we can rest assured that He will always pick us up when we fall. So the next time you experience a defeat, don't get too discouraged—just pray and seek God's strength and wisdom.

Day 69

Supporting Your Teammates

"If your gift is serving others, serve them well. If you are a teacher, teach well."
Romans 12:7, NLT

Whether you're on a sports team, working on a group project, or just hanging out with your friends, it's important to be a good teammate. Good teammates serve one another by supporting and respecting each other's goals and opinions.

Supporting your teammate means being there for them when they need you. It means helping them achieve both your group's and their individual goals. Whether it's cheering them on from the sidelines or lending a hand with a project, your support can go a long way toward helping your teammates succeed.

In addition, respecting your teammates' opinions is very important. Just because someone has a different opinion than you do doesn't mean that their opinion is wrong. It's okay to disagree with each other, but it's important to do so respectfully. Remember, even though you may not always see eye-to-eye, you're still on the same team.

Finally, it's important to be understanding of your teammates' situations. Everyone has different circumstances that they're dealing with in their lives, and it's important to be understanding of that. If a teammate is going through a tough time, be there for them and offer whatever support you can.

We all need someone to lean on from time to time, and being a good teammate means being there for your friends when they need you most.

BOYS
BIBLE
DEVOTIONS

PART 9

Knowing God

Day 70

God as a Father

"Because you are his sons, God sent the Spirit of his Son into our hearts, the Spirit who calls out, 'Abba, Father.'"
Galatians 4:6, NIV

Do you ever look up at the stars at night and feel small? That's because they are huge! But did you know that there is something even bigger than the stars? God is so big that he made them all. And he knows everything about each one of them. But isn't it amazing that the same God who made the stars is our Father?

God created everything, and He has the power to control everything. But even though He is so great and powerful, He still wants to be our Father. He loves us so much that He sent His Son, Jesus Christ, to die for our sins. When we accept Jesus Christ as our Savior, we become children of God. That means that we are part of His family, and He will always love us and care for us.

As children of God, we can go to him with all of our problems. He will always love us and be there for us, no matter what. So don't be afraid to talk to God, because he is your loving Father. Instead, always think about how privileged you are to have God as your Father.

BOYS

BIBLE

DEVOTIONS

Day 71

Forgiving and Patient

"The Lord is not slow to fulfill his promise as some count slowness, but is patient toward you, not wishing that any should perish, but that all should reach repentance."
2 Peter 3:9, ESV

Imagine you did something really bad. Something so bad that you're sure everyone hates you and will never forgive you. Maybe you lied, cheated, or stole something valuable.

Now imagine that there's one person in the world who knows exactly what you did - and they still love you and want to be your friend. That's how God is. No matter how many times we mess up, no matter how bad our sins are, God is always willing to forgive us.

And not only does He forgive us, but He also promises to forget about our sins completely. That's amazing grace!

Because God is patient and forgiving, we, as Christians, should also be patient with people, especially when they make us angry or upset. Everyone makes mistakes, so we should try to be understanding of others, just as we hope they will be understanding of us.

God is very patient with us, even though we sometimes make choices that disappoint Him. He knows that we are learning and growing, and He wants to give us time to figure things out.

In the same way, we should try to be patient with others and forgive them when they make mistakes. Everyone is on their own journey in life, and we can all benefit from a little patience and understanding.

Day 72

God, Your Provider

"And my God will meet all your needs according to the riches of his glory in Christ Jesus."
Philippians 4:19, NIV

Did you know that one of God's names is Jehovah Jireh? Jehovah Jireh means "God our Provider." And that's exactly what He is! God provides for His children in so many ways. He gives us food to eat, a place to live, clothes to wear, and people to love. Let's take a look at some of the ways God has provided for us.

One of the ways God has provided for us is by giving us food to eat. Every day, we wake up and have breakfast, lunch, and dinner. We might not always like what we're eating, but there's always something to eat! That's because God is our Provider and He knows what we need.

Another way God has provided for us is by giving us a place to live. We might not have the biggest house or the fanciest car, but we have a roof over our heads and a bed to sleep in. That's more than some people have! Again, it's because God is our Provider and He knows what we need.

Finally, God has also provided for us by giving us people to love. We have family members who love us and friends who are there for us. We even have pets who bring us joy! It's because God loves us and He knows that we need love too.

BOYS

BIBLE

DEVOTIONS

He Disciplines His Children

*"My son, do not despise the Lord's discipline or be
weary of his reproof, for the Lord reproves him whom
he loves, as a father the son in whom he delights."*
Proverbs 3:11-12, ESV

Many people think that when God disciplines us, it means He is mad at us. But that's not true! Just like any good parent, God loves His children and only wants what's best for them. That's why He corrects our mistakes early on, so we can learn from them and grow into faithful adults.

God disciplining us is actually a sign of His great love for us. Just like any good parent, He wants to see us succeed in life and become everything He created us to be. So when we make a mistake, He lovingly corrects us so we can learn from it and do better next time.

God has many ways of disciplining His children. Sometimes He allows us to experience natural consequences for our choices, such as getting a bad grade when we don't study for a test. Other times, He may directly intervene in our lives to teach us a lesson, such as taking away our phone privileges when we use it too much. But no matter how He does it, you can be sure that God's discipline is always motivated by love.

Next time you find yourself being disciplined
by God, remember that it's because He loves
you and only wants the best for you.

Day 74

He is Faithful

"Behold, I am with you and will keep you wherever you go, and will bring you back to this land; for I will not leave you until I have done what I have promised you."
Genesis 28:15, NKJV

Have you ever made a promise to someone and then not followed through? Maybe you said you would help your little sister clean up her toys, but then you went outside to play with your friends instead. Or maybe you told your mom you would take out the trash, but then you forgot.

If we break our promises, people will start to worry that we can't be trusted. They may not want to ask us for help anymore, or they may not believe us when we say we will do something.

God is different. He is always faithful. That means we can trust him to do what he says he will do.

He has never broken a promise, and he never will. God has proved to be faithful in the past, and we should be confident that he will do what he says he will do.

When we pray, God hears us and he answers our prayers according to his perfect plan. We may not always understand why things happen the way they do, but we can trust that God is always faithful.

BOYS
BIBLE
DEVOTIONS

Knowing His Voice

*"Therefore, as the Holy Spirit says, "Today, if you hear
his voice, do not harden your hearts as in the rebellion,
as on the day of testing in the wilderness..."*
Hebrews 3:7-8, HCSB

As Christians, we believe that the Holy Spirit speaks to us and guides us. When we feel the Holy Spirit's leading, it's important to listen and not harden our hearts. But how do we know if it's really the voice of God? Well, that's a little bit different for everyone. But there are some things that are universally true.

First of all, God speaks to us through His Word. The Bible is full of guidance and direction for our lives, and when we read it, God uses it to speak to us. He can also speak to us through other people. When we are around other Christians, they can share words of wisdom or encouragement from God that are just for us. And sometimes, God speaks to us directly through our thoughts and feelings.

If you have a sense that you should or shouldn't do something, it might be God trying to guide you. So how do you know if it's really God speaking? The best way is to pray about it and ask Him to make His will clear to you. He will always answer us if we ask Him with a sincere heart. So don't be afraid to listen when the Holy Spirit speaks - He has some great things in store for you!

PART 10

Guiding Principles

Faith

"For in it the righteousness of God is revealed from faith for faith, as it is written, "The righteous shall live by faith."
Romans 1:17, ESV

As Christians, we are called to live by faith. But what does that mean, exactly? Living by faith means trusting in God even when things are tough. It means believing that He has a plan for our lives, even when we can't see the light at the end of the tunnel. And it means following His commands, even when it's not easy.

We make decisions based on our strong belief that God will do his promises to us. This doesn't mean that every decision we make will be successful, but we trust that God is good and knows what is best for us.

Additionally, when we make decisions based on our faith, it shows God that we trust him and are willing to obey him even when we don't understand his plan.

This humility pleases God and often results in blessings for us, even if the decisions we make aren't always easy. It also shows that we are willing to put our faith into action.

When we live by faith, we are living like Christ did. And that is the best way to live. So, the next time you're facing a difficult decision, remember to put your faith in Jesus and trust that he will lead you in the right direction.

Love

"Love is patient, love is kind. It does not envy. It does not boast. It is not proud. It does not dishonor others. It is not self-seeking, it is not easily angered. It keeps no record of wrongs."
1 Corinthians 13:4-8, NIV

As Christians, we are called to love one another. But what does that really mean? The Bible tells us that love is patient and kind. That means that even when someone is annoying us or doing something we don't like, we should still show them kindness and not get angry with them.

Love is also sacrificial, which means that sometimes we will have to put others' needs above our own. For example, if a friend is sad and we know they would feel better if we gave them a hug, even though we might not feel like it, we should do it anyway because it would be an act of love.

In addition, the Bible also says that love is not jealous or proud. Love does not demand its own way. It is not irritable, and it keeps no record of wrongs. Love does not rejoice about injustice, but rejoices whenever the truth wins out. Love never gives up, never loses faith, is always hopeful, and endures through every circumstance.

God's love for us is the perfect example of what real love looks like, and He wants us to share that kind of love with others.

BOYS

BIBLE

DEVOTIONS

Purity

"Blessed are the pure in heart: for they shall see God."
Matthew 5:8, ASV

Have you ever wondered what God looks like? Some people say that He is an old man with a long white beard, but the Bible tells us that nobody has ever seen God. So how can we see Him? The Bible says that the only way to see God is to have a pure heart. That means being kind and good, even when it's hard. It also means forgiving others when they hurt us.

A pure heart will allow us to go to God with a clean conscience. When our hearts are pure, we can approach God with confidence, knowing that He will hear us and answer our prayers. Additionally, a pure heart is essential for living a joyful and fulfilling life. When our hearts are free from impurity, we are better able to focus on God and His plan for our lives.

Additionally, a pure heart allows us to be more loving and compassionate toward others. When we are not bogged down by sinful thoughts and desires, we are better able to show Christ's love to those around us.

Finally, a pure heart is a testimony to the power of God's forgiveness. When we have been forgiven by God, it gives us the strength to forgive others and start fresh with a clean slate.

Day 79

Speech

"Let your speech be always with grace, seasoned with salt, that ye may know how ye ought to answer each one."
Colossians 4:6, ASV

As Christians, we are called to speak with grace. This means that we should always think about how our words might affect others. If we say something hurtful, it can damage relationships and leave emotional scars. That's why it's so important to think before we speak. We should always ask ourselves if our words will bring joy or pain. If they will lift someone up or tear them down.

When you are thinking about what to say, always remember to use grace. That means being extra careful not to hurt someone's feelings. Even if you don't mean to, words can sometimes hurt more than we realize. Imagine how you would feel if someone said something mean to you - it probably wouldn't feel very good.

So, try to think about how others might feel when you're speaking, and always choose kind words instead of hurtful ones. By using our words wisely, we can show others the love of Christ and build them up instead of tearing them down. So the next time you're tempted to say something hurtful, remember to speak with grace.

BOYS

BIBLE

DEVOTIONS

Day 80

Good Conduct

"Only conduct yourselves in a manner worthy of the gospel of Christ, so that whether I come and see you or remain absent, I will hear of you that you are standing firm in one spirit, with one mind striving together for the faith of the gospel."
Philippians 1:27, NASB

As a Christian, you represent Christ to the world. That means that people should be able to see Christ in you by the way you behave and treat others. It's important to conduct yourself in a way that is worthy of the gospel at all times. That doesn't mean you're perfect - we all make mistakes. But it does mean that you are striving to act like Christ in every situation.

You can do this by controlling your anger and other emotions which can make you lose your cool. Try not to hurt other people's feelings. But be loving and gracious when you deal with all kinds of people. In the same way, keep your feet on the ground even when you're very excited and happy.

Always try to please God and be sensitive to what others might feel. When people see the Light of Christ shining through you, it will help them to see Him more clearly and maybe even want to know Him for themselves. So don't underestimate the power of your witness - always try to show Christ's love to others in everything you do!

Self-Control

"Like a city whose walls are broken through is a person who lacks self-control."
Proverbs 25:28, NIV

When you get mad, you can be compared to a city with walls that are falling down. Mad feelings are like an unstoppable force. But just like a city, if you let your walls fall down, you're vulnerable to all sorts of trouble. That's why it's so important to learn how to control your emotions.

As Christians, we are called to exercise self-control in all areas of our lives. It means that we need to be in control of ourselves and not let our emotions or desires take over and control our thoughts, words, and actions.

So, we really need to think about our words and actions before we do or say them. We also need to resist temptation and make good choices, even when it's hard.

When we do that, we show that we are following God's plan for our lives and that we are living according to His Word. With self-control, we become like a city with strong walls: We can withstand anything that comes our way.

When you feel like you are losing control, take a step back and pray for God's help. He will give you the strength you need to exercise self-control and live a godly life.

BOYS

BIBLE

DEVOTIONS

Day 82

Joy

"Rejoice always, pray continually, give thanks in all circumstances; for this is God's will for you in Christ Jesus."
1 Thessalonians 5:16-18, NIV

Can you command emotions? Can you just tell someone, "Hey, be happy!" This might come as a surprise to you, but God actually commands us to "rejoice always."

How do we actually make ourselves feel joy, especially when things don't go our way? We can do this by being grateful and by consciously finding reasons to thank God for. Even on your saddest days, there are still a lot of things to be happy about. For example, imagine your parents said you couldn't go to your friend's house for the weekend. Although this is very disappointing, you can still try to appreciate what your parents have planned for you instead. Maybe you have some yard work to do, or you're all visiting your Grandparents. You can appreciate these other activities and be happy with the people you're with, even though that was not your original plan.

When disappointing or bad things happen, you can still be happy because the true source of your joy is God, Himself! Rejoicing in God is a way of worshiping Him. The next time you are feeling sad or upset, remember to ask God to help you rejoice. He will give you His joy, and you will be able to praise Him no matter what happens!

Peace

"Peace I leave with you; my peace I give you. I do not give to you as the world gives. Do not let your hearts be troubled and do not be afraid."
John 14:27, NIV

There are a lot of things in this world that can upset you or make you worried. But if you remember that Jesus is always with you, you can find a kind of peace that nothing else can give you.

First, when you know Jesus is with you, you don't have to be afraid of anything because he will take care of you. Jesus also gives us his peace when we ask for it. That means that even when things are tough and we're feeling stressed out, we can ask Jesus to help us feel better.

When we're feeling lost, scared, or alone, we can go to Him and He will help us find our way. He will give us the strength to keep going, even when things are tough.

Lastly, when we have the peace of Jesus in our hearts, we can share it with others. When we act like Jesus and show love and forgiveness to others, we help them find the same kind of peace that we have found.

So next time you're feeling upset or worried, remember that Jesus is always with you and that he can give you the kind of peace that the world can't offer.

BOYS

BIBLE

DEVOTIONS

Day 84

Perseverance

"Let us not become weary in doing good, for at the proper time we will reap a harvest if we do not give up."
Galatians 6:9, NIV

We all face tough times. Maybe you're struggling in school or you're having a hard time making friends. Maybe you're going through a family issue or you're dealing with something difficult at home. Whatever the situation, it's important to remember that we can persevere through tough times because we are God's beloved children.

When things are tough, it can be tempting to give up or to take the easy way out. Sadly, some people tend to give up or turn away from God when they encounter problems. However, the Bible tells us that we must not grow weary in doing good. This only shows that life will not always be easy. There will be times when we are faced with challenges and obstacles.

Sometimes, we even get disappointing results no matter how hard we try to achieve a goal. However, if we trust in God and keep our focus on him, we can overcome anything.

When you're feeling discouraged, remember that God wants what's best for you. He will help you become a better person and He's happy to shower you with blessings and successes. But sometimes, He wants us to undergo difficulties so we can learn important lessons in life. So don't give up-keep pressing on toward the goal!

PART 11

My Journey
with God

Day 85

Reading God's Word

"Your word is a lamp for my feet and a light on my path."
Psalms 119:105, HCSB

The Bible is like a map. It directs our steps so that we would know where to go. And in this verse, the Bible is compared to a lamp because it helps us find the path we should take, especially when we're in the dark. So, as Christians, it's very important to read God's Word. Otherwise, it would be very easy to get lost and forget God's teachings.

The Bible guides us in many ways. When we hear the Bible stories, we can understand how much God loves us. We see how He provided for His people and protected them from their enemies. We learn about how God works in amazing ways from these stories. In addition, we can read about God's power to heal the sick. He even raised the dead! This can give us hope when we need God to help us when we need Him most.

By reading the Bible, we also get to know Jesus better. We see how He lived a perfect life on earth and then died on the cross for our sins. We learn about his love, his patience, and the good example he set for us to follow.

So, let's make sure to read our Bibles every day so that we can grow closer to God and learn more about His wonderful plan for our lives!

Obeying God

"For this is the love of God, that we keep his commandments: and his commandments are not grievous."
1 John 5:3, ASV

As Christians, we believe that God is the creator of the universe and everything in it. He is all-powerful and all-knowing, and His will is perfect. As His children, we are called to obey Him and follow His commands.

The Bible is our guidebook for life, and it contains everything we need to know about how to live according to God's will. God's commands can sometimes be difficult, especially when we don't understand why He wants us to do something.

Some unbelieving people would even say that the Bible's teachings are unfair, just because those teachings don't support their ideas or desires. But if you look into God's will closely, you'll understand how He wants us to be pure and loving, just like Jesus.

So, when we don't understand some of His commands, we can trust that He knows what is best for us. When we obey Him, we show our love and respect for Him. After all, He is God, and He deserves our highest worship and obedience. And as we grow in our relationship with Him, He will reveal His plans to us little by little. So let's remember to always obey God, no matter what.

BOYS

BIBLE

DEVOTIONS

Day 87

Praise and Worship

"Let everything that has breath praise the Lord. Praise the Lord."
Psalm 150:6, NIV

Do you enjoy singing praises to God? Doesn't it just help you express your love for God? When you praise and worship God, you speak to God through music.

This is also like praying and you are communicating with God. You are telling Him how amazing He is! You are also acknowledging that He is holy, powerful, and deserving of every creation's worship. When you praise and worship God, you are expressing your thankfulness for all the good things in your life.

By raising your voice in praise, you are also opening your hearts to receive His love and grace. That is why you feel like your heart is filled with joy when you sing.

Sometimes, though, worshipping doesn't just mean singing. Instead, you can also worship God by being quiet and just thinking about Him. You can also worship God by obeying Him in your life.

Worshipping God is one of the most important things you can do as a Christian because it shows that you love and trust Him.

So when you next sing praises to God, remember that you are doing more than just singing words on a page. You are joining your voice with the chorus of believers who have gone before you, and you are proclaiming the glory of God for all the world to hear.

107

Following God's Plan

"Many plans are in a man's heart. But the counsel of the Lord will stand."
Proverbs 19:21, NASB

People often have great plans for their lives. Our plans and dreams encourage us to do our best every day. Maybe you want to be a teacher, a businessman, or even the president of the United States! But as you grow older, you'll realize that your plans don't always align with what God has in store for you. And that's okay! In fact, it's better than okay – it's best to always follow God's will over your own plans.

God's will is best because He is the all-knowing God. No matter how much you plan and prepare, there will always be things that are out of your control. That's why it's important to remember that God is ultimately in control of your life, and He knows what's best for you even when you don't.

While your plans may not always work out, you can trust that God has a perfect plan for your life. His plan is better than anything you could ever hope or dream for yourself!

Following His will ensures that you will end up exactly where He wants you to be. Moreover, you'll find true happiness when you live a life that is in alignment with God's will for you.

When you try to go your own way, you will end up feeling lost and confused. But when you surrender your plans to God and let Him lead the way, you'll find true peace and happiness.

BOYS

BIBLE

DEVOTIONS

Glorifying God

*"So, whether you eat or drink, or whatever
you do, do all to the glory of God."*
1 Corinthians 10:31, ESV

No matter what you do, you are commanded to do all for the glory of God. But why is that? Why can't you just do whatever you wish to do? If you're constantly thinking about how everything you do reflects on God, it will keep you from getting a big head.

It's easy to start thinking you're better than others when you're doing well. But if you remember that it's all for God's glory, it will help you stay humble. Next, doing everything for God's glory helps you make good decisions.

When you're trying to decide whether or not to do something, ask yourself if it will bring glory to God. If the answer is no, then chances are you shouldn't be doing it.

In addition, knowing that everything you do is for God's glory will motivate you to always give your best effort. You'll want to do things that will make Him proud and show His love to others through your actions. Finally, glorifying God in everything you do is an act of worship.

You don't only worship God when you're at church or when you're praying or singing. Instead, your whole life should be an offering to God. Live in a way that glorifies God, even to the tiniest detail, because God sees what's in your heart.

Day 90

Sharing Jesus' Love

"And he said to them, 'Go into all the world and proclaim the gospel to the whole creation.'"
Mark 16:15, ESV

How did you get to know about God? Is it because you were born into a Christian family? Or did someone reach out to you? Even if you've grown up in a church, there's a good chance your parents or grandparents heard about God from someone who were concerned about their souls.

The truth is that people come to know God when someone else shares the gospel with them. And once you receive God's gift of salvation, it's your task to share the gospel with others who may not know Jesus yet. Jesus is very clear in His command for us, Christians, to go and make disciples of all nations. When we share the gospel with others, we obey what Jesus has asked us to do.

Moreover, we need to share the gospel because people need to hear about Jesus.

We live in a fallen world, and because of that, everyone needs a Savior. When we share the gospel with others, we are giving them an opportunity to hear about Jesus and learn about His love for them.

Finally, when people come to know Christ as their personal Savior, it brings glory to God. As Christians, our ultimate desire should be to glorify God in everything we do. When we share the gospel with others, we give glory to our God.

BOYS
BIBLE
DEVOTIONS

Day 91

Let Your Light Shine

*"In the same way, let your light shine before others,
so that they may see your good works and give
glory to your Father who is in heaven."*
Matthew 5:16, ESV

The Bible compares us, Christians, to a light. And we are called to let our light shine before men. This means that we should be living our lives in such a way that others can see Christ in us and be drawn to Him. It can be easy to get caught up in the things of this world and forget our purpose, but if we keep our focus on God, He will help us to shine His light on those around us.

One way you can let your light shine is by being kind to others. When you show kindness, you are showing the love of Christ. Others will see that love, and it will be a testimony for them. Another way to let your light shine is by being obedient to your parents and other adults.

When you obey, it shows that you respect authority and that you are willing to follow God's commands. This also shows that you are respectful, which pleases God very much. Others will see your obedience, and it will be a testimony for them as well.

On the other hand, if you are rude and disrespectful, others will feel like you're no different from those who don't follow God. But when you let your light shine, others will see Christ in you, and they may even come to know Him as their Savior too! So don't be afraid to let your light shine!

111

PART 12.

Becoming a Man

Day 92

The Right Role Model

"And do not be conformed to this world, but be transformed by the renewing of your mind, so that you may prove what the will of God is, that which is good and acceptable and perfect."
Romans 12:2, NASB

There's a lot of pressure to be like everyone else, even when you're a Christian. It can be easy to get caught up in what the world is doing and start following their lead instead of Jesus'. But that's not what God wants for us! He wants us to be different, to stand out, and to be a light in the darkness. And the best way to do that is by making Jesus our role model.

Above everyone else, Jesus should be our role model because he is perfect. There's nobody else in the world who can say that they lived a perfect life, but Jesus did. He never sinned, no matter how tempted he was.

If we want to be like Jesus, we need to strive for perfection, too, even if we might fail many times. We should also follow Jesus' example as he always sought to help people. He healed the sick, fed the hungry, and comforted the brokenhearted. If we want to be like Jesus, we must also consider others first.

So, instead of following someone who may be full of human flaws, fix your eyes on Jesus and follow in His footsteps.

Day 93

Seek Maturity

*"Therefore, let us move beyond the elementary teachings
about Christ and be taken forward to maturity, not
laying again the foundation of repentance from
acts that lead to death, and of faith in God."*
Hebrews 6:1, NIV

As a kid, you're not just growing physically; you're also growing emotionally and spiritually. Physical growth is something that happens naturally. But you will need to work on your emotional growth. Yet, the bigger question is: how do you make sure you'll grow spiritually too?

The first way to spiritual growth is going back to God's Word. Read your Bible regularly. This will help you learn more about God and His plan for your life. You can start by reading a few verses every day and then eventually work up to reading whole chapters. By going through this devotional every day, you are already on the right track to spiritual maturity.

Another important way to grow in your faith is to pray often. This is how you communicate with God and tell Him what's going on in your life. You can pray anytime and anywhere - when you wake up in the morning, before you go to bed at night, while you're in the car, and everywhere else. Just take a few minutes each day to talk to God and tell Him what's on your heart.

More importantly, try to listen to what God wants you to learn in every situation. Growing in your faith isn't something that happens overnight - it's a lifelong journey that requires effort and dedication.

BOYS

BIBLE

DEVOTIONS

Day 94

Keep your Word

"Therefore each of you must put off falsehood and speak truthfully to your neighbor, for we are all members of one body."
Ephesians 4:25, NIV

A man is only as good as his word. This is an age-old saying that has been passed down from generation to generation for a reason. In the Bible, we'll see a lot of verses telling us to keep our word. This is because a man who cannot keep his word is not a man at all—he is a boy.

And even though you may still be a boy, it's important that you start learning how to be a man of honor right now. Sometimes, boys might be able to get away with breaking their promises, but men cannot. If you want to be respected as a man, you need to learn to keep your word. When you give your word, you are also making a promise. And when you make a promise, people are going to expect you to keep it.

Whether you are promising to do something big or small, your word should always mean something. If you say you're going to do something, do it. If you can't do it, don't say you're going to in the first place.

So, keep your promises and never break them unless necessary because you're not just some boy You are God's representative in this world.

Day 95

Standing Firm

"Be watchful, stand firm in the faith, act like men, be strong."
1 Corinthians 16:13, ESV

It can be tough to stand up for what you believe in, especially when it goes against what everyone else is doing. But that's exactly what Jesus calls us to do: to be different and to be a light in the darkness. And that's not always easy.

Jesus was often confronted by people who didn't agree with Him. People thought He was crazy. People thought He was wrong. But He never backed down from what He knew was right. And neither should we. When Jesus was on Earth, He often found Himself in situations where He had to stand firm in His beliefs. And even though it wasn't always easy, He never backed down from what He knew was right. As a child and when you become a teenager, you will be faced with so much peer pressure. Other kids might encourage you to do things just so you can be "cool" like them. But remember, their idea of cool may not be really cool. It might just be plain wrong.

So next time you're faced with a situation where you have to choose between doing what's popular or doing what's right, remember Jesus and His example of standing firm in your beliefs—no matter what anyone else says or does.

BOYS

BIBLE

DEVOTIONS

Day 96

Accepting Consequences

"For he who does wrong will receive the consequences of the wrong which he has done, and that without partiality."
Colossians 3:25, NASB

Growing out of childhood, it's important to always think before you act. That's because every decision you make has consequences, both good and bad. And as a man, it's your responsibility to accept the consequences of your actions, even if they're not what you wanted or expected.

Consequences are a natural part of life. They're the result of the choices we make, both good and bad. And while we can't always control the consequences of our actions, we can control our actions themselves. That's why it's so important to always think before you act.

Every decision you make has consequences. Some of those consequences might be positive—like getting a good grade on a test because you studied hard. But some of those consequences might be negative—like getting a bad grade on a test because you didn't study at all.

It's not always easy to deal with the consequences of our actions, especially when they're negative. But as a man, it's your responsibility to accept them nonetheless. That doesn't mean you have to like them, but it does mean that you have to learn from them and try not to repeat the same mistakes in the future.

Integrity

"To do what is right and just is more acceptable to the LORD than sacrifice."
Proverbs 21:3, NIV

Integrity is often described as "doing the right thing even when no one is watching." In other words, it's about being honest and truthful, even when it's difficult. People of integrity are known for being reliable and trustworthy. So how can you grow up to be a man of integrity?

First, be honest with yourself. This means being aware of your own thoughts, feelings, and actions. If you're not honest with yourself, it will be difficult to be honest with others. The second step is to be honest with other people. This means speaking the truth, even when it's hard to do so. It also means being reliable and keeping your promises.

People who are dishonest often end up disappointing others or getting into trouble. Finally, stand up for what you believe in, even when it's not popular or easy to do so. This might mean standing up for someone who is being treated unfairly, or speaking out against something that you think is wrong.

It takes courage to do this, but it's important to stand up for what you believe in if you want to be a person of integrity. As you can see, integrity is really a combination of different values. So, to be a man of God, always seek to be honest and stand up for what is right. Wear integrity like a medal of honor.

BOYS

BIBLE

DEVOTIONS

A Healthy Sense of Humor

"A joyful heart is good medicine, but a
crushed spirit dries up the bones."
Proverbs 17:22 ESV

"Laughter is the best medicine," an old saying says. It's one of those things that make life more fun. And in today's verse, we also see a confirmation that laughter is, indeed, a good medicine. Science shows us how laughter relaxes our muscles and releases endorphins, which make us feel good. It also helps us to see the funny side of things and not take life too seriously.

So, what does all this mean for us? It means that having a sense of humor is something that God wants us to have. It's not something that we should try to force or fake. Instead, we should thank God that He made us, humans, with a good sense of humor. And when we do laugh, we should remember that it's good for us!

Some people are just naturally funny, but that doesn't mean that you can't develop your sense of humor. For example, instead of getting mad when someone accidentally spills their drink on you, try to see the funny side of it and laugh it off.

Remember, laughter is contagious—so once you start laughing, chances are good that others will start laughing too! A sense of humor is a valuable asset to have! Not only does laughter have some great benefits for your physical health, but it also helps you connect with other people. Instead of getting upset when something goes wrong, you can, instead, allow your sense of humor to kick in from time to time.

Day 99

Getting Serious

"A time to weep, and a time to laugh; a time to mourn, and a time to dance."
Ecclesiastes 3:4 ESV

There are lots of different times when you need to be serious. For example, if you're at school, you need to be paying attention and doing what you're supposed to do. If someone asks you a question, you need to answer it seriously.

You can't just laugh and joke around all the time. Sometimes people might get hurt if you're not being serious. If you're joking around all the time, people might not take you seriously when you're trying to be serious. They might think you're just joking around even when you're not.

Knowing when to be serious is important because it shows that you're grown up and responsible. People will trust you more if they know that you can be serious when you need to be.

So when is the right time to stop joking around and start being serious? There are a few key times in life when it's important to put away the jokes and start acting like a grown-up. It could be when you're in church, at a formal event, or when you're at school. When you're being serious in these situations, you're being respectful by listening when others are talking. This is also especially true when you're talking to a friend who wants to confide with you.

When you sense that the other person has something important to say, be a good listener and don't just laugh it off.

BOYS

BIBLE

DEVOTIONS

Day 100

Confidence in God

*"Such confidence we have through Christ before God. 5
Not that we are competent in ourselves to claim anything
for ourselves, but our competence comes from God."*
2 Corinthians 3:4-5, NIV

Confidence is something that a lot of people struggle with. While a lot of people might tell you that you have to be confident because you're perfect and amazing, the Bible tells you that your confidence shouldn't come from your own strength. Instead, you should be confident because of who your God is.

When it comes to confidence, people often think about being sure of yourself or your abilities. But where does this confidence come from? As a Christian, your confidence should come from God because He is the source of our strength. You can be confident, knowing that God loves you very much and He wants what's best for you.

When you are going through tough times, you can be confident that God is using those difficult circumstances to make you grow into maturity.

So, if you're struggling with confidence, remember that you can be confident because you are a child of God! Lean on Him and trust Him to help you through whatever situation you may be facing.

PART 13

I Am Unique

Day 101

Dreams for a Better Future

"Jabez cried out to the God of Israel, 'Oh, that you would bless me and enlarge my territory! Let your hand be with me, and keep me from harm so that I will be free from pain.' And God granted his request."
1 Chronicles 4:10, NIV

Just like Jabez, you can pray to God for a better future. After all, God owns everything, and He has the power to make your future really great. And just as He did with Jabez's prayer, He can also grant your dreams for a better future.

When you dream of a better future, you're asking God to help you. You're telling God that you want to be great. Just like Jabez, you're asking for His blessing. And when you ask God for His blessing, you're giving yourself a great opportunity to receive those blessings. God wants you to be great. He wants you to have good dreams and goals. When you ask Him to help you, He will bless you with what you need to achieve your dreams.

Sometimes, though, God may give you challenges along the way as a way of strengthening your faith so you would be ready to receive these great blessings. Sometimes, God would also withhold some things if what you're asking for will make you bad or turn away from Him.

So keep on seeking God's will and praying for your heart's desires. Don't be afraid to ask God for help in achieving your dreams. He wants to bless you and make your dreams come true!

Developing a Positive Attitude

"Get rid of all bitterness, rage and anger, brawling and slander, along with every form of malice. Be kind and compassionate to one another, forgiving each other, just as in Christ God forgave you."
Ephesians 4:31-32, NIV

A lot of people think that being a good Christian is all about going to church on Sundays and reading the Bible. While those things are important, they're not the only things that make up a good Christian. One of the most important things you can do to grow as a mature Christian is to develop a good attitude.

Your attitude has a huge impact on your life. If you have a positive attitude, you're more likely to see the good in people and situations. You're also more likely to be successful in whatever you do because you believe in yourself and your ability to achieve your goals. On the other hand, if you have a negative attitude, you're more likely to see the bad in people and situations. You're also more likely to give up on your goals because you don't believe in yourself. Developing a positive attitude isn't always easy. It's something that you have to work on every day.

So, before you even start your day, it's important to pray and think about the attitude that God wants you to have have a grateful, joyful, and loving heart for God and for everyone you will meet throughout the day.

BOYS

BIBLE

DEVOTIONS

Day 103

Building Healthy Self-Esteem

"Are not two sparrows sold for a penny? Yet not one of them will fall to the ground outside your Father's care. And even the very hairs of your head are all numbered. So don't be afraid; you are worth more than many sparrows."
Matthew 10:29-31, NIV

Have you ever felt like you're not special? Sometimes, you may feel less special, especially when you compare yourself to others. But the truth is, you are special in God's eyes. He created you and knows everything about you. He knows the good things you have done and the bad things too. And he still loves you.

In fact, he loves you so much that he was willing to sacrifice his one and only Son, Jesus, to save you from your sin. You are special to God because he made you. Just like every snowflake is different, every person is different too. And just like every snowflake is beautiful, every person is beautiful too. God doesn't make mistakes, so that means he made you exactly the way he wanted to. And he wants to use your unique talents and abilities for his purposes.

Now that you know how special you are, it's time to start acting like it! Be confident in who God made you to be. Don't compare yourself to other people because nobody is exactly like you. Trust that God has a plan for your life and follow his leading one day at a time. When you do these things, God will use you in amazing ways!

125

Appreciating My Privileges

*"Give thanks in all circumstances; for this is
God's will for you in Christ Jesus."*
1 Thessalonians 5:18, NIV

We all have privileges. Some more than others, but we all have them. It's important to remember that your privileges are not something you should take for granted. They're gifts that you should appreciate. First of all, you have a family who takes care of you.

Your parents or guardians are the people who care and provide for you. They work hard to make sure you have everything you need. They love you and want what's best for you. So, show them some appreciation by being grateful for everything they do for you.

Another privilege you have is that you can go to school. Not everyone has the opportunity to go to school and get an education. But you're blessed to go to school and learn new things every day. So, be thankful for that privilege and make the most of it. Also, be thankful for the roof over your head and the food on the table.

Even when you don't really like the food, these are still blessings you should be thankful for. But most importantly, you are privileged to worship God freely. In some countries, people are not allowed to worship God freely. They may be persecuted or even killed if they try to practice their religion openly.

So, if you get to go to church or even just speak about Jesus with others, do those things with a grateful heart.

BOYS

BIBLE

DEVOTIONS

Day 105

My Unique Self

"Yet you, Lord, are our Father. We are the clay, you are the potter; we are all the work of your hand."
Isaiah 64:8, NIV

Have you ever wished you were someone else? Maybe you thought someone else was better or cooler. But what you may forget is the fact that you are awesome just the way you are. You are unique! God created you as his handiwork.

There's nobody else like you. You were made to be special and to do special things. God made you look the way you do on purpose. He gave you your own special combination of hair color, eye color, and skin color. He made you exactly the height and weight you are. He even gave you your own special fingerprints!

God also gave you a brain that is wired in a unique way. You think about things differently than anyone else does. Your unique perspective is one of the things that makes you special.

In addition, God has given you a combination of talents and abilities that one else has. You might be good at sports, art, music, math, science, writing, or other things. Whatever it is, use your talents to glorify God and help others!

Finally, you are uniquely you because of your experiences. You've been through some things in your life that no one else has been through. Maybe you've faced some challenges.

Whatever it is, your experiences have shaped who you are today, and they make you unique. Celebrate your uniqueness and use it to glorify God and help others!

127

Day 106

My Imperfections

That is why, for Christ's sake, I delight in weaknesses,
in insults, in hardships, in persecutions, in difficulties.
For when I am weak, then I am strong.
2 Corinthians 12:10, NIV

Having faults and weaknesses isn't great. Sometimes, our own weaknesses can stop us from being successful at something. But to be great, we don't need to be perfect. In fact, it's better to not be perfect. Why? Because when we're not perfect, we have room to grow. We can learn from our mistakes and become better people as a result.

One of the best ways to learn and grow is to identify our weaknesses and then work on them. One way to identify your weaknesses is by paying attention to what other people say about you. If you keep hearing the same thing from multiple people, chances are there's some truth to it. For example, if people keep telling you that you're always late, chances are you need to work on punctuality.

Once you've identified your weaknesses, you can start working on them by setting specific goals for what you want to achieve. For example, if you want to get better at math, set a goal of getting a certain grade on your next math test or completing a certain number of math problems in a certain amount of time. Try to get help from others and be patient with yourself.

Also, it's very important to persevere through setbacks. Don't give up on yourself because God won't either. God will help you with your weaknesses if you ask him to.

BOYS

BIBLE

DEVOTIONS

Popularity

"Whoever walks with the wise becomes wise, but the companion of fools will suffer harm."
Proverbs 13:20, ESV

It can be tempting in school to try to be friends with everyone. But it's more important to be friends with the right people. The people who you are friends with will have a big influence on you. So it's better to be friends with kids who will be a good influence on you, even if they are not popular.

Being friends with the right people means being friends with people who have similar values as you. It means being friends with people who will make you a better person. These are the kind of people who will challenge you to be your best self. They are the kind of people who will support you and help you when you need it. It's important to be friends with the right people because they will have a big influence on you. The things that your friends do and say will affect how you think and how you behave.

If your friends are always getting into trouble, then there's a good chance that you'll get into trouble too. But if your friends are doing well in school and behaving like good citizens, then there's a good chance that you'll do well in school and be a good citizen too.

And if you have Christian friends, then you can help keep each other on the right track and be easily swayed by peer pressure.

Day 108

The Enemy's Lies

"For the word of God is alive and active. Sharper than any double-edged sword, it penetrates even to dividing soul and spirit, joints and marrow; it judges the thoughts and attitudes of the heart."
Hebrews 4:12, NIV

The devil doesn't want us to be happy or to know God for who He is. All day long, he whispers lies in every mind. But you don't have to fall for his tactics! The Bible is full of truth that can help remind you of what is real and what is false.

Every time you have negative thoughts, take a moment to ask yourself: does this line up with what God says in His Word? If not, then you can be confident that it's nothing but a lie from the enemy.

Study God's word and remember what He says. When the enemy whispers to you, "You are weak," remember that Isaiah 40:31 says that in God, you are strong.

When the enemy says, "You are not important," tell yourself the truth: "I am God's treasured possession." (Deuteronomy 7:6). When the enemy says, "You are a failure!" Refute him with Romans 8:37 and say, "No! I am more than a conqueror!" When the devil tells you, "You are rejected!" You can fight back with the truth from Ephesians 1:6 and say, "No! In Jesus, I am accepted."

BOYS

BIBLE

DEVOTIONS

God Loves Me

"As the Father has loved me, so have I loved you. Now remain in my love."
John 15:9, NIV

Can you imagine someone so powerful, amazing, and perfect to love you very, very much? It may be hard to wrap your head around the concept of the all-powerful God loving you, specifically. I mean, there are billions of people in the world. How could God possibly love every single person all the same? But that's the beauty of it, really.

God's love is immense and eternal. It's not based on our actions or our words. It's simply there for us to accept or reject. And that's the most amazing thing of all. That we have been given this great gift of love, and it's up to us what we do with it.

As Jesus says in today's verse, He loves us. Yes, you are loved. Look at how God has blessed you. He will keep blessing you if you remain in His love.

Today, take some time to think about all the ways God has blessed you. Maybe He has given you a great family, good health, or a pet that you love.

Whatever it is, be thankful for it and for the God who gives you everything you need. So, never ever feel that nobody loves you or that you are not special. The God of the universe loves you very, very much!

PART 14

When I am In Trouble

Day 110

Take Refuge in God

*"God is our refuge and strength,
an ever-present help in trouble."*
Psalm 46:1, NIV

Have you ever got lost in a crowded place? It's always scary when we find ourselves in an unfamiliar place or when we are facing something we've never faced before. But it's when we feel scared that we find strength in God. It's when we're in trouble that we need to remember that God is our refuge.

A refuge is a place of safety or protection. We all have times in our lives when we feel like we need a refuge - a place to hide from the storm, so to speak. For some people, their home is their refuge. For others, it might be a quiet spot in nature. And for many people, their faith is their refuge. In times of trouble, they turn to God for comfort and strength. The Bible tells us that God is our "refuge and strength, an ever-present help in trouble."

When we put our trust in Him, we can find peace and safety in His love. We can always seek Him out when we're feeling scared or alone. He will be our strength and He will never fail us.

Instead of being afraid, we need to put our trust in God and know that He will see us through whatever situation we're facing. We need to remember that He is always with us and He will never leave us alone.

Day 111

God Hears You

"And if we know that he hears us—whatever we ask— we know that we have what we asked of him."
1 John 5:15, NIV

One of the best things in life is having a friend you can always enjoy talking to. They make you laugh, they listen to you, and they're just generally fun to be around. It's the same with God - when you pray, you're talking to your friend. And just like any good conversation, it should be enjoyable.

Don't feel like you have to pray a certain way or use big words. Just talk to him like you would your best friend. Tell him what's going on in your life, how you're feeling, and what you're thankful for. And take time to listen too. Prayer isn't just about talking; it's about listening to what God has to say to you. So take some time each day to enjoy talking to your friend God. It'll make your relationship with him even stronger.

Even if you don't think you're worthy, always pray to God. He sees your heart and knows your intentions. If you're sincere, He will take delight in listening to your prayers. No matter what your circumstances are, don't give up hope and always turn to Him.

He's always there for you, even when it feels like no one else is. So don't be afraid to pour your heart out to Him, because He loves you unconditionally.

BOYS
BIBLE
DEVOTIONS

134

Day 112

Hold Fast to Hope

"We must hold on to the hope we have, never hesitating to tell people about it. We can trust God to do what he promised."
Hebrews 10:23, ESV

Life isn't always easy. There will be times when you feel like giving up, when it feels like the whole world is against you. But don't lose hope. Hold fast to the hope that things will get better. Because they will. While feeling discouraged is normal, what's not okay is staying discouraged. That's when you start to lose hope and give up on your dreams. And that's when you need to remember that God is always there for you.

Remember that God is the same powerful and loving God of the future as He is now. And He hasn't given up on you. So don't give up on yourself either. Keep going, even when it feels like everything is against you. Because eventually, you will make it through to the other side. And when you do, remember that God was with you the entire time.

He gives us hope for a better future. Not just a future here on Earth, but an amazing future that we can't even imagine in heaven.

So when things seem tough and you start to feel down, just remember that God is with you and He has great things in store for you. Keep the faith and never give up hope.

When Tears Flow

"For his anger lasts only a moment, but his favor lasts a lifetime; weeping may stay for the night, but rejoicing comes in the morning."
Psalm 30:5, NIV

Have you ever met a person without any problem? Try to imagine someone with a perfect life? What do you think would be that person's problems. I can imagine that you can still think of a possibility for that person. The truth is that problems are a fact of life. They're like roadblocks that prevent us from reaching our goals. But it's important to remember that problems are meant to help us grow. They help us to learn and experience God's love.

It's just really wonderful to be a Christian because we have a God who will turn our tears into joy. It means that even when you are going through something bad right now, you can be sure that your life isn't always going to stay bad. You just have to persevere through that and learn what God wants you to learn through that situation.

Just like the darkness of night is followed by the light of day, our problems will eventually be replaced by happiness and success. So don't give up when you face difficulties. Remember that they're only temporary. And trust that God will see you through to the other side.

BOYS

BIBLE

DEVOTIONS

Day 114

From Bad to Good

"And we know that in all things God works for the good of those who love him, who[a] have been called according to his purpose."
Romans 8:28, NIV

It's easy to trust God when things are going well. We feel His blessings and we are confident in His love for us. But what about when things are tough? When we face difficult times, it can be tempting to doubt that God is good. We may even start to question whether He really loves us.

Sometimes, we may feel scared because of different circumstances. But a lot of times, our worries don't actually happen. In fact, things could turn out even better than we could have ever imagined. And that's because God has a plan for us. He can use even the bad situations in our lives to give us positive results.

He knows what we need, even when we don't. And He always has our best interests at heart. So when we face challenges, let's remember that God is still in control. He is faithful and all-powerful. If we keep our faith in Him and ask for His help, He will rescue us from trouble.

All you need to do is to come to God and tell Him everything. Of course, He already knows what's going on. But He wants you to draw close to Him and learn to trust His goodness. You will be amazed when you witness Him turn everything for your good in the end.

PART 15

Prayer Life

Day 115

Why We Pray

"Is anyone among you in trouble? Let them pray. Is anyone happy? Let them sing songs of praise."
James 5:13, NIV

As Christians, we believe that God created us in His image and blessed us with many talents and abilities. We are often quick to use our own intelligence and resourcefulness to find solutions to problems. However, this can sometimes lead to arrogance and a sense that we don't need God.

It's easy to stop praying to Him when we feel like we can rely on ourselves. But the truth is that we should always be praying, regardless of our circumstances. Prayer is our way of communicating with God and showing Him that we need His help. When we pray, we humble ourselves before Him and acknowledge His power and goodness.

As a young Christian, it's very important that you develop the habit of praying. It's your way of spending time with your Father in Heaven. But most of all, praying gives you the opportunity to connect with God, himself. And that's the most wonderful privilege granted to us as children of God.

So, even when things are going well, never forget to pray always, giving thanks to God for all His blessings. And when you're in need, let your requests be made known to God so you can be a recipient of God's special blessings to those who pray.

Day 116

Asking in Faith

*"But when you ask, you must believe and not
doubt, because the one who doubts is like a wave
of the sea, blown and tossed by the wind."*
James 1:6, NIV

Sometimes, you may have feelings of doubt or fear when you pray. Sometimes, you may even be wondering if God is really listening or if He will grant you what you ask for.

However, the Bible tells us that we should have faith when we pray. Believe that God wants to grant you what is good for you. He is happy when He sees you believing in Him. So always ask in faith.

This doesn't mean that you will always get everything you want. But it does mean that God will always give you what is best for you. Sometimes we can't see how something could be good for us, but we trust that God knows better than we do.

He loves us and wants what is best for us, even if it means saying no to our prayers sometimes. Pray with faith, knowing that God is always listening and He wants to help us grow closer to Him.

Jesus tells us that if we have faith and do not doubt, we will be able to move mountains. This doesn't mean that God will give us everything we want; instead, it means that He will grant us what is good for us.

So when you pray, have faith that God knows what you need and that He wants to give you His best.

BOYS
BIBLE
DEVOTIONS

Day 117

Waiting on the Lord

*"But they that wait upon the Lord shall renew their strength;
they shall mount up with wings as eagles; they shall run,
and not be weary; and they shall walk, and not faint."*
Isaiah 40:31, KJV

Have you ever looked up at the sky and seen how fly eagles fly? They soar to great heights, effortlessly gliding on currents of air. For many people, watching an eagle in flight is an awe-inspiring experience. But did you know that there is a lesson to be learned from these majestic birds?

Just as eagles fly high above the mountains and hills, waiting on the Lord's will in your life can help you to achieve new heights as well. When you are patient and trust in God's plan for your life, you will be able to overcome any obstacle.

But how do we wait on the Lord? Whenever you have to make a decision, it is always important to consult with God first and ask for guidance. This is what we mean when we say "waiting on the Lord."

It means taking the time to pray and listen for His direction instead of just rushing into things on our own. He will speak to us through our thoughts and feelings, giving us a "go" signal when we are headed in the right direction.

So it's important to take some time each day to quiet our minds and hearts, so we can hear His voice more clearly.

God Says Yes

*"Call to Me, and I will answer you, and show you great
and mighty things, which you do not know."*
Jeremiah 33:3, NKJV

If you've ever wondered if God hears your prayers, the answer is a resounding yes! Throughout the Bible, we see many examples of how God answered the prayers of His people.

For instance, in the book of Psalms, we read about how God rescued King David from his enemies. In the book of Exodus, we see how God led the Israelites through the desert using a pillar of fire and a cloud.

And in the New Testament, we read about how Jesus healed people and performed other miracles in response to people's prayers.

But you don't have to look to the Bible to find examples of answered prayer. Just ask your parents or grandparents about times when they prayed for something and saw God work in their lives. Chances are they have lots of stories to share! Their testimonies are an encouragement for you to never stop praying, especially when you encounter problems. You should call out to Him and tell Him everything that's on your mind, even if it's something you're embarrassed about.

You can trust that He will listen to you and help you, because He loves you. And even when it seems like your prayers aren't being answered, you shouldn't give up.

Remember that God's ways are higher than ours, so sometimes He knows what's best for us even when we don't. Just keep trusting in God and don't ever give up on Him, and He will never give up on you.

Day 119

Be Still

"Be still, and know that I am God; I will be exalted among the nations, I will be exalted in the earth!"
Psalm 46:10, NKJV

When you're in trouble, it's easy to panic. The heart races, the mind races, and it feels like everything is spiraling out of control. But it's important to remember that, even in the darkest moments, God is in control.

He sees your situation, and He knows what's best for you. So take a deep breath and relax, knowing that He has everything under control. Don't allow fear to control your thoughts. Instead, quiet your thoughts down and just spend some time with God.

You don't have to kneel or sit down in quiet to be talking to God. He hears the whispers of your heart. You can talk to God when you're happy, when you're sad, when you're scared, or when you just need someone to listen. It's okay to tell God everything that's on your mind. He already knows what's going on, but he wants to hear it from you. And he will always listen.

Just remember that he is always there for you, no matter what. Once you are reminded, then focus on the task at hand and do your best. Trust that God will lead you through whatever challenges come your way.

Day 120

A Time with God

"As the deer pants for streams of water, so my soul pants for you, O God. My soul thirsts for God, for the living God. When can I go and meet with God?"
Psalm 42:1-2, NIV

At last, you've reached the last day of our devotional. How do you feel every time you finish one passage? How do you feel when you meditate in God's truths and then come to Him in prayer? Doesn't it feel fulfilling? That's because reading God's word and meditating on His truths feed our souls.

Deep within you is a thirst for God because you are created to worship and love Him. If you spend time with God, His Spirit communes, or speaks, with your spirit. And when you worship Him in your heart, you are fulfilling your purpose for being alive.

The Lord of lords, our Creator, is what our empty hearts desire. Only God can satisfy our deepest desires.

So, later in life, if you feel like you're in the dark and you sense that something is missing in your life, remember this: Your soul is thirsty for God, and anything else that's not God will never fully fill your emptiness. But if you abide, or stay close, to Jesus, your heart will always be filled with joy, faith, and other fruits of the Spirit.

So, no matter what your schedule looks like, always find some time in the day to spend quality time with God. God bless you, and may you have a wonderful life with our Lord and Savior, Jesus Christ.

BOYS

BIBLE

DEVOTIONS

Conclusion

Congratulations on finishing this devotional. Throughout the book, we talked about your identity in Christ, your relationship with God, Salvation, and your daily walk with God. I hope you've learned a lot and have been blessed by reading this book. It is my prayer that you would keep the habit of reading God's word and setting a special time with Him every day. Have a blessed life!

Printed in France by Amazon
Brétigny-sur-Orge, FR

20455382R00087